JOURNAL FOR THE STUDY OF THE NEW TESTAMENT
SUPPLEMENT SERIES
175

Executive Editor
Stanley E. Porter

Sheffield Academic Press

Naming Jesus

Titular Christology in the Gospel of Mark

Edwin K. Broadhead

Journal for the Study of the New Testament
Supplement Series 175

Published by Sheffield Academic Press Ltd
Mansion House
19 Kingfield Road
Sheffield S11 9AS
England

Printed on acid-free paper in Great Britain
by Biddles Ltd
Guildford, Surrey

British Library Cataloguing in Publication Data

A catalogue record for this book is available
from the British Library

ISBN 1-85075-929-4

To

Jessica Loftis
(1979–1993)

and to

John Loftis
(1951–1993)

Scholar, Colleague, Friends

CONTENTS

This work seeks to provide a responsible reading of one stream of primitive theology. This investigation is a 'reading' in that it offers a descriptive analysis controlled by the parameters of the text. This reading seeks to be responsible by holding in view both the historical foundations and the theological implications of the text.

While each analysis begins with a sketch of the historical background to that title, comprehensive statements are impossible within this context. In similar fashion, this study is not yet a constructive theology grounded in the titles; it is a preliminary statement undergirding this task. The investigation that follows should be read as a descriptive analysis of literary patterns and strategies employed in the naming of Jesus within the Gospel of Mark. While this reading demonstrates its connections to historical and theological tasks, its ultimate concern is the naming of Jesus within stories of faith.

The initial framework of this study was sketched in the midst of an extended rail journey through Scandinavia. These *en route* sketches were solidified within the more traditional academic settings of study and classroom in Zürich and Melbourne. Final changes were made in Mississippi and Kentucky. Hopefully this work will prove as well informed as it is well traveled.

I am grateful for those who have helped me on my way. Many thanks and much gratitude are due to Loretta Reynolds, my spouse and co-minister. She has demonstrated much patience in the sharing of our home and much vision in the sharing of our dreams.

I remain grateful for the encouragement of Mark Brett, my former colleague in Biblical Studies at Whitley College of Melbourne, Australia, and for the wider support of the Fellowship of Biblical Studies of Melbourne. Dean Harold Pidwell of the Melbourne College of Divinity has proven to be a capable administrator and an extraordinary friend. I salute my students at Whitley who aided the development of these ideas through their patient listening and probing questions. I am also grateful for the support offered by my present employer, Berea College, in the final stages of this work.

I also salute my teachers, who have not only provided information and challenge, but have also served as models for my own ministry of instruction. Among those who have so deeply enriched my life and work are Frank Stagg, Eduard Schweizer, Hans Weder, Ulrich Luz, Jean Zumstein, Peter Stuhlmacher, Martin Hengel, Jürgen Moltmann, Alan Culpepper, John Polhill, James Blevins, George Beasley-Murray, Robert Shurden, Ruth Morris, Cathy Caldwell.

This text is dedicated to John Loftis, a gifted historian, and to his daughter Jessica. They perished together in the flames; they remain in our memories and in our hopes. Compassionate realism and unconditional friendship were his gifts to me. They are deeply loved, sorely missed, often remembered.

Luther compared the Church to a drunken man riding home late at night upon a donkey: first he sways to the left, then to the right, constantly drawing near to disaster. Then at last, only by the grace of God, the pilgrim makes it home. May this work in some way aid the Church, of which I am a part, on its arduous journey.

ABBREVIATIONS

AB	Anchor Bible
ABD	David Noel Freedman (ed.), *The Anchor Bible Dictionary* (New York: Doubleday, 1992)
BDF	Friedrich Blass, A. Debrunner and Robert W. Funk, *A Greek Grammar of the New Testament and Other Early Christian Literature* (Cambridge: Cambridge University Press, 1961)
BZ	*Biblische Zeitschrift*
CBQ	*Catholic Biblical Quarterly*
FRLANT	Forschungen zur Religion und Literatur des Alten und Neuen Testaments
HNT	Handbuch zum Neuen Testament
HTKNT	Herders theologischer Kommentar zum Neuen Testament
JBL	*Journal of Biblical Literature*
JBLMS	*Journal of Biblical Literature*, Monograph Series
JJS	*Journal of Jewish Studies*
JSNTSup	*Journal for the Study of the New Testament*, Supplement Series
JSOT	*Journal for the Study of the Old Testament*
NTS	*New Testament Studies*
OTP	James Charlesworth (ed.), *Old Testament Pseudepigrapha*
RB	*Revue biblique*
SBL	Society of Biblical Literature
SBLSP	SBL Seminar Papers
Str-B	[Hermann L. Strack and] Paul Billerbeck, *Kommentar zum Neuen Testament aus Talmud und Mishnah* (7 vols.; Munich: Beck, 1922–61)
TDNT	Gerhard Kittel and Gerhard Friedrich (eds.), *Theological Dictionary of the New Testament* (trans. Geoffrey W. Bromiley; 10 vols.; Grand Rapids: Eerdmans, 1964–)
ZNW	*Zeitschrift für die neutestamentliche Wissenschaft*
ZTK	*Zeitschrift für Theologie und Kirche*

Chapter 1

INTRODUCTION

> Then came Jesus and his disciples into the village of Caesarea Philippi.
> And in the way he was asking his disciples, saying to them, 'Who are
> people saying that I am?'...And he asked them, 'But you, who are you
> saying that I am?' (Mk 8.27-29).

It is the task of the Church to give form, structure and coherence to the
experience of faith. It must speak of the unspeakable, drawing upon the
language, concepts and images at hand. It is the task of critical scholarship to analyze the processes through which the Church describes its
faith. Both tasks are inexhaustible; both are inescapable.

The Quest for the Christological Titles

From its inception critical scholarship has sought to clarify the significance of christological titles—the names given to Jesus. These titles
prove central for the history of Jesus, for the faith of the early Church,
and for the formulation of New Testament theology. The development
of this research represents an ongoing dialectical quest between history
and dogma.

*THESIS: The key to the christological titles, as to all christological
dogma, lies in the consciousness of Jesus. There is a one-to-one correlation between the dogmatic value of the titles and Jesus' use of these
terms.*

Pre-Enlightenment hermeneutics understood the christological titles and
other christological expressions as Jesus' direct self-conscious identification of himself. Thus, there was perceived to be a one-to-one correlation between Jesus' self-understanding and the dogma of the Church
about Jesus. The christological titles were perceived within this hermeneutic: Jesus was the Messiah because he thought and spoke of himself
as such.

The first major challenge to this union of history and dogma was presented in the works of Herrmann Samuel Reimarus (1694–1768).[1] Reimarus, a teacher of Oriental languages in Hamburg, constructed a critique of Christianity from the viewpoint of a radical Deism. This was intended as a personal document to address his own questions. After the death of Reimarus his work was published in seven anonymous fragments by Gotthold Ephraim Lessing. Reimarus drew a sharp line between the teaching of Jesus and the message of the apostles. He sought 'completely to separate what the apostles present in their writings from what Jesus himself actually said and taught during his lifetime'.[2] Reimarus evaluated the divide between Jesus and his followers negatively. He argued that Jesus preached the nearness of the messianic kingdom wholly from a Jewish secular perspective. Upon the death of Jesus the disciples, intent on worldly power and privilege, invented the idea of a spiritual figure who redeems all of humanity. For Reimarus this vision was accomplished by their theft of the corpse of Jesus and their subsequent proclamation of his resurrection as the savior of humanity. These events meant that only a few traces of the authentic Jesus could be found in the Gospels. The impact of Reimarus's position is clear: the various claims posed by the christological titles were seen to belong to the dogma of the Church rather than to the teaching of Jesus.

This challenge fell most heavily upon the Fourth Gospel, for it is here that Jesus speaks most clearly in christological terms. Consequently the search for the Jesus of history was reduced to the synoptic Gospels, and eventually to the Gospel of Mark.

The challenge laid down by Remairus set the agenda for the Liberal Quest of the nineteenth century. The task of the quest was to separate the authentic religion of Jesus from the dogmatic formulations of the Church. Whereas pre-Enlightenment thought had associated all christological dogma with the proclamation of Jesus, the Liberal Quest sought to isolate the pure religion of Jesus from the ecclesiological dogma imposed upon him. The quest typically pointed to a worldly ethical religion which sought to generate the kingdom of God upon earth. In

1.   The work of Reimarus is discussed by W. Kümmel, *The New Testament: The History of the Investigation of its Problems* (trans. S. Gilmour and H. Kee; Nashville: Abingdon Press, 1972 [1970]), pp. 89-90.

2.   Cited in Kümmel, *History*, p. 89.

this way the quest sought to re-establish the direct connection between the authentic proclamation of Jesus and dogmatic constructions.

The quest met its sharpest critique in the work of Albert Schweitzer. Building upon the earlier work of Johannes Weiss, Schweitzer insisted the images of Jesus generated by the quest represented the ethical impulses of modern writers more than those of Jesus:

> The Jesus of Nazareth who came forward publically as the Messiah, who preached the ethic of the Kingdom of God, who founded the Kingdom of Heaven upon earth, and died to give His work its final consecration, never had any existence. He is a figure designed by rationalism, endowed with life by liberalism, and clothed by modern theology in an historical garb.[3]

Nevertheless, Schweitzer believed the historical consciousness of Jesus could be recovered. Schweitzer insisted that Jesus must be understood within his own world as one driven by a thoroughgoing eschatology. The secret messiahship of Jesus is to be explained in terms of his view of the coming kingdom. Consequently Schweitzer called for renewed faith in the Gospel presentations of the messiah: the messianic secret is rooted in the historical consciousness of Jesus. For Schweitzer, Jesus comes to understand that he is indeed Son of God, Messiah, the Son of Man soon to be revealed. The mystery of this identity, as Jesus discovered, was linked to his suffering and death: 'Within the secret of the Passion lay concealed the secret of the Kingdom.'[4] In this way Schweitzer sought to re-establish the continuity between certain christological titles and the self-consciousness of Jesus.

The presumption that the christological titles and images of the synoptics represent the proclamation of Jesus was taken up in various forms. In pre-Enlightenment hermeneutics the dogma about Jesus was founded upon his own concepts, and this view continues in various non-critical interpretations. Following upon the challenge of Reimarus, the Liberal Quest attempted to isolate the terms which represented the pure religion of Jesus. Johannes Weiss and Albert Schweitzer found in the eschatological view of the Gospels the authentic self-identity of

---

3.   Albert Schweitzer, *The Quest of the Historical Jesus: A Critical Study of its Progress from Reimarus to Wrede* (trans. W. Montgomery; London: A. & C. Black, 2nd English edn, 1911 [1906]), p. 396.

4.   Albert Schweitzer, *The Mystery of the Kingdom of God: The Secret of Jesus' Messiahship and Passion* (New York: Macmillan, 1950 [1901]), pp. 160-73.

Jesus. A few titles and images are still seen by some as direct expressions of Jesus' consciousness. Thus, many interpretations of Christianity—both critical and non-critical—see a direct correlation between the faith of the Church and Jesus' use of christological titles.

ANTITHESIS: The key to christological titles, as to all christological dogma, lies in the Church and its articulation of the faith experience.

The other side of Reimarus's divide was taken up by numerous interpreters. In these positions the christological titles and images are expressions of the believing Church imposed upon the historical Jesus. Reimarus evaluated this thesis negatively and characterized the activity of the apostles as motivated by worldly and materialistic concerns. In contrast to the position of Reimarus, Martin Kähler saw this divide as a positive element. For Kähler, Jesus could be known only as the Christ of faith proclaimed through the early Church. Isolated facts gleaned from the history of Jesus could not motivate the faith of the Church. Kähler argued that faith had an 'invulnerable area' in the dogmatic or christological authority of the Bible. He insisted that the key was not the *historische Jesus* reconstructed through the life of Jesus research, but rather the *geschichtliche, biblische Christus*, the Christ of the whole Bible. The most vital description of this historic Christ is not to be found in the seemingly historical elements of the Gospels, but rather in the confession of Jesus as the crucified and risen Lord. For Kähler the Gospel narratives about Jesus are the product and reflection of Christian faith, not its source:

> Thus, our faith in the Savior is awakened and sustained by the brief and concise apostolic proclamation of the crucified and risen Lord. But we are helped toward a believing communion with our Savior by the disciples' recollection of Jesus, a recollection which was imprinted on them in faith...[5]

In this manner Kähler sought to ground all christological dogma in the faith experience of the Church.

The negative position articulated by Reimarus and the positive reformulation of this position by Kähler provide theoretical frameworks for interpretation of Jesus and early Christianity. These theoretical frameworks were subsequently developed through exegetical studies which attempted to separate the history of Jesus and christological dogma.

5.   Martin Kähler, *The So-Called Historical Jesus and the Historic, Biblical Christ* (trans. C. Braaten; Philadelphia: Fortress Press, 1964 [1892]), pp. 96-97.

The most influential of these exegetical studies was provided by William Wrede in 1901.[6] Wrede believed that the messianic identity of Jesus first emerged in the post-resurrection confession of the Church. Since the Gospel writers could not legitimately convey a messianic lifestyle for Jesus, Mark framed the story of Jesus under the guidance of a messianic secret: Jesus was not revealed as messiah in his lifetime because he chose to keep his identity a secret until the point of the resurrection. The confession of Jesus as messiah and other christological dogma thus belong to the post-resurrection faith of the Church and not to the facts of Jesus' life.

Wilhelm Bousset confirmed this division from a history of religions perspective in 1913.[7] For Bousset christological titles and christological dogma emerge primarily in the faith of the early Church, which borrowed these terms from Judaism and other religious traditions. Bousset thus argued that the Son of Man title was borrowed by the Church from Jewish apocalyptic thought and applied to Jesus:

> One cannot avoid the impression that in the bulk of the Son-of-man sayings we have the deposit of the theology of the primitive church. That is the certain and given point of departure. All that is uncertain is whether and to what extent a few of the Son-of-man sayings are to be traced back to Jesus...[8]

A similar situation is seen behind the designation of Jesus as the Lord:

> It lay, so to speak, in the air that the first Hellenistic congregations of Christians should give their cult hero the title 'Lord'...*Kyrios*-faith and *Kyrios*-cult represent the form that Christianity assumed on the soil of Hellenistic piety.[9]

Bousset then traces the development of further christological titles and images within the worlds of Paul and of the Fourth Gospel.

---

6.   William Wrede, *The Messianic Secret* (trans. J.C.G. Greig; Cambridge: James Clark, 1971 [1901]).

7.   Wilhelm Bousset, *Kyrios Christos: A History of the Belief in Christ from the Beginning of Christianity to Irenaeus* (trans. J. Steely; Nashville: Abingdon Press, 1970 [1913]).

8.   This citation is from Kümmel, *History*, p. 271. Kümmel works from an earlier version than the translation by Steely.

9.   Cited in Kümmel, *History*, p. 273.

A similar position was articulated by Wilhelm Heitmüller shortly before the appearance of Bousset's *Kyrios Christos*.[10] Heitmüller argued that the course of development ran from Jesus to the primitive community to Hellenistic Christianity to Paul. He believed that the designation of Jesus as the Lord did not arise within the primitive community, but within Hellenistic Christianity.

Martin Dibelius combined both history of religions concerns and literary analysis in his investigation of early Christianity. Working from this perspective, Dibelius attempted to show how Paul developed his Christology against a mythical background drawn from Hellenistic thought. In his treatment of the Gospels, Dibelius asserted that Mark created a Christology which addressed the tension between Jesus' wondrous deeds and his scandalous death: 'Mark solved this contradiction by his theory of the Messianic secret. He put not only the great miracles but the whole activity of Jesus under the standpoint of a secret epiphany.'[11] Clearly the impetus for this Christology lies with Mark.

Rudolf Bultmann located the significance of christological titles and dogma precisely in the preaching of the early Church. He was convinced that the few facts that could be known about the historical Jesus were of little relevance for faith. In the opening lines of his *Theology of the New Testament* Bultmann insisted that '*The message of Jesus* is a presupposition for the theology of the New Testament rather than a part of that theology itself'.[12] For Bultmann Christian faith did not exist until the preaching of Jesus Christ as the crucified and risen one, and this proclamation occurs first in the kerygma of the earliest Church, not in the message of the historical Jesus.[13] Bultmann was most concerned to show that a messianic consciousness on the part of Jesus was not a necessary element for faith, even if such consciousness could be proven to exist. For Bultmann

> the acknowledgment of Jesus as the one in whom God's word decisively encounters man, whatever title be given him—'Messiah (Christ),' 'Son of Man,' 'Lord'—is a pure act of faith independent of the answer to the

---

10. W. Heitmüller, 'Zum Problem Paulus und Jesus', *ZNW* 13 (1912), pp. 320-37.

11. Martin Dibelius, *From Tradition to Gospel* (trans. B. Woolf; Cambridge: James Clarke, 1971 [1919]), p. 297.

12. Rudolf Bultmann, *Theology of the New Testament* (2 vols.; trans. K. Grobel; London: SCM Press, 1952 [1948]), I, p. 3.

13. Bultmann, *Theology of the New Testament*, I, p. 3.

historical question whether or not Jesus considered himself the Messiah. Only the historian can answer this question—as far as it can be answered at all—and faith, being personal decision, cannot be dependent upon a historian's labor.[14]

In this way Bultmann ascribes, in positive fashion, the entire christological program to the activity of the believing Church. Like Bousset and Heitmüller before him, Bultmann believed the christological titles were borrowed primarily from the history of religions.

Bultmann's assertion that christological dogma is the work of the believing Church and not of Jesus was grounded in three critical perspectives. From his form-critical investigations Bultmann concluded that the traditions were formed primarily in the life settings of the early Church; from a history of religions perspective he concluded that these concepts and titles were largely borrowed from other religious traditions; from a theological perspective he concluded that faith need not—indeed could not—be founded on the historian's work.

The division between the mission of Jesus and the message of the Church was sketched in a negative way by Reimarus and given positive status in the thought of Kähler. Kähler's theoretical position was given exegetical support in the work of various scholars. Consequently the christological titles were seen as faith formulations emerging within the life of the earliest Church. These terms were drawn largely from the religious world surrounding Christianity and were applied to Jesus as expressions of faith in the crucified and risen Christ.

SYNTHESIS: The New Quest: The christological titles are Church formulations based on faith, but this faith is rooted in the history of Jesus.

The theoretical divide between history and dogma was stated from a negative perspective by Reimarus, transformed into a positive theological principle by Kähler, then given exegetical support in the work of Bultmann and others. Various attempts to bridge this divide may be noted.

While form-critical studies made it extremely difficult to look for Christology prior to Easter, many scholars did not abandon the attempt.[15] Prior to the New Quest, scholars such as T.W. Manson and

---

14. Bultmann, *Theology of the New Testament*, I, p. 26.

15. This movement is discussed by John Reumann, 'Jesus and Christology', in E. Epp and G. MacRae (eds.), *The New Testament and its Modern Interpreters* (Atlanta: Scholars Press, 1989), pp. 501-506.

William Manson continued to appeal to eyewitness sources or traditions. The thought of Adolf Schlatter survived in the work of Ethelbert
Stauffer in Germany.[16] Joachim Jeremias continued to pursue material
in the Gospels that goes directly back to Jesus.[17] A group of Scan-
dinavian scholars—H. Riesenfield, B. Gerhardsson, T. Boman—argued
for scribal practices which ensured the continuity between the message
of Jesus and that of his followers. Each of these efforts attempted, in
the face of Bultmann's three-pronged program, to connect the teaching
of Jesus to the Christology of the Church.

The most important attempt to bridge the divide while maintaining its
distinctions was articulated from within the Bultmannian school.[18] Ernst
Käsemann issued the challenge in 1953 to Bultmann's students and
friends. Käsemann contended that a new quest for Jesus was both scien-
tifically possible and theologically necessary. He believed that distinctive features of Jesus' ministry—such as his sovereign freedom and
authority—could be isolated without falling into the dangers of the life
of Jesus research. Käsemann's call encouraged those who had never
abandoned the search, and it provided a new impetus for work on the
life of Jesus.

Günther Bornkamm's *Jesus of Nazareth* provided the most important
response to this call. Bornkamm's position demonstrates the synthetic
nature of this movement: he argued that Jesus made a deliberate decision to go up to his death in Jerusalem, but none of the christological
titles goes back to Jesus. Other scholars pursued this task to differing
degrees. The New Quest remained directly influential through the
1960s, and its indirect influence continues through to the present.

Beyond the Synthesis
The decades following the New Quest synthesis have been marked by
two streams of study on the christological titles. One stream attempts to
sort through the various titles in order to demonstrate the roles of Jesus
and the Church in the formulation of New Testament Christology.
Under the impact of redaction criticism, another stream focuses on the

---

16. See E. Stauffer, *New Testament Theology* (trans. J. Marsh; London: SCM
Press, 1955 [1941]).

17. See J. Jeremias, *The Problem of the Historical Jesus* (trans. N. Perrin;
Philadelphia: Fortress Press, 1977 [1964]).

18. See the discussion by Reumann, 'Jesus and Christology', pp. 508-509.

ways in which individual authors of the Gospels employed titles in their theological programs.

Titles in New Testament Theology. Several studies surveyed the titles in an attempt to map the christological thought of early Christianity. In these studies attention is given to the history of religions development of titles within and beyond Judaism. The possible use of the title by Jesus himself is considered. Primary attention is given to stages of Christian development and to the ways in which various titles were used to articulate faith in Jesus. Four such surveys may be highlighted.

1. Oscar Cullmann's *Die Christologie des Neuen Testaments* appeared in 1957. In his quest for a 'total picture of the Christological conceptions of the New Testament'[19] Cullmann analyzed the development of individual titles. He divided his survey into four theological categories which represent stages of salvation history: titles which refer to the earthly work of Jesus (Prophet, Suffering Servant, High Priest), titles which refer to the future work of Jesus (Messiah, Son of Man), titles which refer to the present work of Jesus (Lord, Savior), titles which refer to the pre-existence of Jesus (the Word, Son of God, God). Reflecting the model of Bultmann, Cullmann draws simultaneously upon the history of religions background of each term, upon its role in early Christian life, and upon its theological impact.

Cullmann insists that 'All Christology is founded upon the life of Jesus'.[20] He seeks to isolate various concepts active in the consciousness of Jesus and the manner in which these concepts were expressed in titles. Cullmann argues that the baptism of Jesus initiated in him a consciousness of carrying out God's plan. His awareness that he must bring forgiveness through his death is a fulfillment of the prophecy of the Suffering Servant. His announcement of the kingdom of God and his life of lowliness connect with the Son of Man title. His 'complete and unique oneness with God'[21] undergirds the title of Son.

While the veiled allusions of Jesus did not raise the christological question among his disciples in his own lifetime, they were eventually confronted with the significance of the teaching and activity which they had witnessed. In this manner the Church sought out titles which would

19. Oscar Cullmann, *The Christology of the New Testament* (trans. S. Guthrie and C. Hall; London: SCM Press, 1963 [1957]), p. 6.
20. Cullmann, *Christology*, p. 317.
21. Cullmann, *Christology*, p. 318.

clarify their experience with Jesus. Initial efforts by the followers drew from Jewish categories such as the eschatological prophet or the messianic king. It was the experience of the cross and the resurrection which most stirred the christological reflection of Jesus' followers. Various christological titles came into use in the dialectic between the hope of Jesus' future coming and the remembrance of his previous coming: Servant of God, Son of Man, Lord.

This anchoring of faith in the present and coming Lord to the life of Jesus of Nazareth provided the foundation from which various other titles emerged. Once this concept of salvation history was in place 'All theology became Christology'.[22] This christological conception of history was then extended to include the pre-existence of Jesus. As Christian missions pushed into the Hellenistic world, numerous external elements impacted its Christology. While various other traditions were appropriated, the origin of Christology is found in the history of salvation at its core. In this manner Cullmann gathers the whole of christological reflection around the concepts of representation and revelation throughout salvation history: 'Therefore all Christology is *Heilsgeschichte*, and all *Heilsgeschichte* is Christology.'[23]

The work of Cullmann invokes the New Quest synthesis, but seeks to move forward through a comprehensive survey to articulate a holistic view of the development of New Testament Christology. Jesus' consciousness emerged in veiled allusions and in a limited use of a few titles, none of which led immediately to christological reflection by his followers. The continuing impact of this contact with Jesus and the experience of the present lordship of the risen Christ allowed the early Church to perceive Jesus' role in God's history of salvation. For Cullmann it was this experience and this perception which generated the wider development of christological titles and of New Testament Christology.

2. Other studies followed in the wake of Cullmann's work. Ferdinand Hahn investigated the development of major titles (Son of Man, Lord, Christ, Son of David, Son of God) in order to clarify the history of their development within early Christianity.[24] Hahn surveys these titles independently, then seeks in conclusion to point to some unifying factors.

22. Cullmann, *Christology*, p. 320.
23. Cullmann, *Christology*, p. 326.
24. Ferdinand Hahn, *The Titles of Jesus in Christology: Their History in Early Christianity* (trans. H. Knight and G. Ogg; London: Lutterworth, 1969 [1963]).

He is convinced that the sayings which point to the future coming of the Son of Man provide the most original Son of Man sayings and that some of these come from the lips of Jesus. Jesus was addressed as Teacher, Master, Lord within his lifetime. These terms refer to his earthly authority and carry no sense of exaltation in their first usage. Hahn believes that all images of a zealotic or kingly messiah are missing from Jesus' activity, and that Jesus likely repudiated the messianic title.[25] The Son of David emphasis was first picked up within the early Palestinian church, as was the Son of God title.

Hahn seeks to trace the larger development of christological titles under the impetus of the future: 'The earliest Christology has in all its distinctive features a consistently eschatological orientation.'[26] The origin of christological tradition is to be found in concepts of the coming Son of Man, the returning Lord, and the Messiah appointed in the last days. Jesus' earthly ministry was first framed in non-messianic images through terms such as Master and Lord. From these points of origin the Palestinian and Hellenistic churches developed wider conceptions of the work of Jesus.

3. Reginald H. Fuller attempted a similar survey of christological development.[27] His investigation of the background of the titles treats their role within Palestinian Judaism, within Hellenistic Judaism and within the Hellenistic Gentile realm. His view of the role of the titles in the self-understanding of Jesus represents a distinct change from his earlier work.[28] Fuller finds an implicit Christology present in Jesus' words and deeds and in some traditions of his death. There is present with Jesus no explicit messianic claim and no display of direct messianic consciousness, but Jesus was conscious of a unique sonship. Jesus did not use the Servant title, he made only a preliminary use of Lord, and the Son of Man sayings originate in Church formulations. Jesus understood himself in prophetic terms, though he did not use Prophet as a self-designation. Fuller thus seeks to root the explicit christological developments of the Church in a Christology implicit in Jesus' life: 'Jesus understood his mission in terms of eschatological prophecy

25. Hahn, *Titles*, p. 161.
26. Hahn, *Titles*, p. 347.
27. R.H. Fuller, *The Foundations of New Testament Christology* (London: Lutterworth, 1965).
28. R.H. Fuller, *The Mission and Achievement of Jesus* (London: SCM Press, 1954).

and was confident of its vindication by the Son of man at the End.'[29]
For Fuller 'It is the unexpressed, implicit figure of the eschatological
prophet which gives a unity to all of Jesus' historical activity...'[30] This
implicit understanding present in Jesus' ministry provides the foundation for explicit christological developments within various stages of
the early Church.

4. Petr Pokorný presents the most recent systematic attempt to cate-
gorize the development of christological titles and dogma.[31] Pokorný
argues that Jesus had a unique awareness about his mission. This
awareness of his prophetic and eschatological role in God's salvation is
revealed in symbolic actions such as his proclamation of the kingdom,
various activity associated with this message, the breaking of bread and
his journey to death in Jerusalem. Pokorný then develops the relationship between this consciousness and the christological titles: 'In the
light of our conclusions about the unique awareness Jesus had about his
mission we are hardly surprised that attempts to prove that Jesus used
the post-Easter Christological titles during his earthly life have been
abortive.'[32] Pokorný ultimately argues that all of the varied christological elements of the New Testament represent a unified stream of tradition which has its genesis in the passion preaching.

In addition to these surveys, numerous studies have given attention to
the development and use of individual titles. These studies typically
seek to demonstrate the history of religions background of a single title,
its use or non-use with Jesus, and its subsequent development in the
thought of the early Church.[33]

29. Fuller, *Christology*, p. 130.

30. Fuller, *Christology*, p. 130.

31. Petr Pokorný, *Genesis of Christology: Foundations for a Theology of the
New Testament* (trans. M. Lefebure; Edinburgh: T. & T. Clark, 1987 [1985]).

32. Pokorný, *Genesis of Christology*, p. 55.

33. Most of these are concerned with the Son of Man title: typical of this dis-
cussion are G. Vermes, *Jesus the Jew: A Historian's Reading of the Gospels*
(London: Collins, 1973); B. Lindars, *Jesus Son of Man: A Fresh Examination of the
Son of Man Sayings in the Gospels* (London: SPCK, 1983); H.E. Tödt, *The Son of
Man in the Synoptic Tradition* (London: SCM Press, 1965 [1959]); E. Sjöberg, *Der
verborgene Menschensohn in den Evangelien* (Lund: C.W.K. Gleerup, 1955); *idem*,
Jesus und der Menschensohn (Festschrift A. Vögtle; ed. R. Pesch and R. Schnack-
enburg; Freiburg: Herder, 1975); Morna Hooker, *The Son of Man in Mark* (London:
SPCK, 1967). Other works of this nature include Martin Karrer, *Der Gesalbte: Die*

Titles in New Testament Literature. Other studies trace the role of titles within a limited literary tradition. These studies typically focus the way in which one Evangelist makes use of certain titles to construct a christological portrait. A number of these studies debate Mark's manipulation of titles in the service of his Christology. Norman Perrin took up the theory of corrective Christology posited by Theodore Weeden,[34] then linked this tension directly to the relationship between two titles: Son of God and Son of Man. For Perrin, Mark employed his resources to combat the *theios anēr* Christology centered around the title Son of God: 'Christologically Mark is concerned to combat a false Christology, most probably of the θεῖος ἀνήρ type, and this he does particularly by his use of Son of Man and by his conscious subordination of the story of Jesus to the passion.'[35] Several scholars pursued this relationship between christological titles. Weeden, Achtemeier and Petersen find in Mark's use of Son of Man a corrective for other christological understandings.[36] Werner Kelber reverses this proposal, arguing that Mark finds no fault with Son of God, but instead corrects a false, apocalyptic understanding of Son of Man.[37] Jack Dean Kingsbury attempts a more balanced, complementary relation between the use of the two titles.[38] In each of these studies primary attention is given to *Mark's*

Grundlagen des Christustitels (Göttingen: Vandenhoeck & Ruprecht, 1990); Christoph Burger, *Jesus als Davidssohn: Eine traditionsgeschichtliche Untersuchung* (Göttingen: Vandenhoeck & Ruprecht, 1970); Rainer Riesner, *Jesus als Lehrer: Eine Untersuchung zum Ursprung der Evangelien-Überlieferung* (Tübingen: J.C.B. Mohr [Paul Siebeck], 3rd edn, 1988). On the pre-existence of Jesus and his role as the Last Adam and as Wisdom, see J.D.G. Dunn, *Christology in the Making: A New Testament Inquiry into the Origins of the Doctrine of Incarnation* (Philadelphia: Westminster Press, 1980).

34. T. Weeden, *Mark: Traditions in Conflict* (Philadelphia: Fortress Press, 1971).

35. N. Perrin, 'Towards an Interpretation of the Gospel of Mark', in H.D. Betz (ed.), *Christology and a Modern Pilgrimage: A Discussion with Norman Perrin* (Missoula, MT: Scholars Press, rev. edn, 1974), pp. 1-78 (38).

36. Weeden, *Traditions in Conflict*, p. 67; P. Achtemeier, *Mark* (Proclamation Commentaries; Philadelphia: Fortress Press, 1975), pp. 41-50, esp. pp. 45-48; N. Petersen, *Literary Criticism for New Testament Critics* (Philadelphia: Fortress Press, 1978), pp. 60-68, esp. p. 63.

37. Werner Kelber, *The Kingdom in Mark: A New Place and a ·New Time* (Philadelphia: Fortress Press, 1974), pp. 21-22, 62-65, 84-85, 132-37, 138-47.

38. J.D. Kingsbury, *The Christology of Mark's Gospel* (Philadelphia: Fortress Press, 1983), pp. 157-79.

application of a christological title, with little reference to the background of the term or its use by Jesus. J. Fitzmyer provides a brief
sketch of Luke's use of christological titles.[39]

Problems That Remain

The quest for the christological titles has followed a circuitous route.
Critical scholarship has wrestled for 230 years with the divide noted by
Reimarus between the teaching of Jesus and the dogma of the Church.
The pre-critical thesis that christological titles and dogma originate in
the consciousness and words of Jesus was soon met by a counter thesis:
christological dogma is the work of the Church. The New Quest represented a synthesis of these positions: christological titles and dogma
are faith expressions from the early Church, but this faith is rooted in
the Jesus of history. The question has been sharpened by the growing
awareness of other religious traditions (especially of Qumran), by the
development of form criticism, and by the advent of redactional studies.
At no point does the discussion lie far from the theological issues at the
heart of Christianity. This limited survey of research on the christological titles points to a number of problems which remain.

First, history of religions studies have provided no simple background for the titles. The initial studies proved stereotypical and bor-
dered on parallelomania. More recent studies on Hellenistic religion,
the impact of Hellenism upon Judaism, and the Qumran documents
demonstrate that New Testament Christology draws more heavily upon
Judaism than previously thought. At the same time, recent history of
religions insights demonstrate that the background of most titles is
more complex than previously imagined. Indeed, the background of
many titles appears irresolvable.

Secondly, attempts to delve into the consciousness of Jesus have
made only a small advance over the psychological portraits of the nineteenth century. The temptation to explain the activity of Jesus in terms
of modern patterns of motivation remains.

Thirdly, attempts to locate any one title unambiguously on the lips of
Jesus have failed. Fourthly, there is a growing awareness that Christology cannot be written exclusively along the lines of the titles. Alongside our limited awareness of their background and their use by Jesus

---

39. J. Fitzmyer, *The Gospel According to Luke* (AB, 28; Garden City, NY: Doubleday, 1981), pp. 197-219.

stands the phenomenon that titles never carried the central christological load. That task belonged rather to confessions, creeds, hymns, sayings and Gospels. The titles come to us as part of narrative packages, and attempts to study them in isolation prove discomforting. There is a growing consensus that Christology must be structured along more holistic lines.

Fifthly, previous studies have failed to adequately treat the narrative role of the titles. Redactional studies provide a step in this direction, yet they remain focused on the intentions of imagined authors. The formal role of titles as narrative constructions has yet to be properly examined.

Finally, the very description of 'christological titles' may now be called into question. This term connotes a well-defined conception which awaited incorporation into the Christian tradition. Careful research will show that none of the titles is inherently christological, and none of them is unambiguous.[40] The idea that Jesus (or the Church) borrowed fixed titles to describe his work is outmoded. It is more likely that Jesus provided the hermeneutic for understanding the titles. Titles become christological only when they are assigned this role within specific social and literary contexts; christological titles exist only as social and literary constructs.[41]

Toward a Titular Christology

The time has come for a further step, particularly in Markan studies. There are no titles that are inherently and indisputably christological. The titles for Jesus are best understood not simply as historical or editorial markers, but as formal elements which operate within a cohesive narrative world. This formalistic approach to the titles does not preclude their use in the history of religions, on the lips of Jesus, in the life of the early Church or in the minds of the Evangelists, but narrative form and function are taken as the *first* key to understanding christological elements of the Gospel of Mark. Mary Ann Tolbert has moved in this direction with her recent work:

40. To say that the Christ title is inherently christological is a tautology with little relevance, as the synoptics demonstrate.

41. The name of Jesus provides a christological title within many modern cultures and texts. In its original context and in some modern contexts it enjoys common usage.

> Recently, the practice of looking at 'titles' has come under increasing
> attack as the difficulty of establishing with certainty a fixed tradition of
> usage and meaning behind any of the 'titles' has become increasingly
> clear. Whether they should be called 'titles' at all is highly debatable...
> In order to discover the specific understanding of Jesus guiding each of
> the canonical Gospels, instead of studying 'titles', a truly narrative Chris-
> tology must be developed that attempts to perceive the distinctive func-
> tion and depiction of the character of Jesus within the dynamics of each
> story... Thus, the Christology of Mark is not established by looking at
> 'titles' provided for Jesus; rather, the meaning of the 'titles' is defined by
> the narrative itself.[42]

While titles may have historical or redactional roles, this analysis will
consider their role as formal literary elements operating within a narrative strategy and a narrative world. This investigation will show how
such elements may serve in focused literary strategies and may produce
sharp narrative images and claims.

This approach to the titles demands a change in terminology. The
perception that titles are pre-packaged conceptual units which may be
called upon to define the role of Jesus is to be rejected. There are no
titles which are inherently and unambiguously christological; they
become so only within defined social and literary contexts. Because of
this recognition, it is perhaps more accurate to speak of 'Titular Christology' rather than 'Christological Titles'. Titular Christology recognizes that the titles, along with various other materials, have been taken
up as strategic elements in the characterization of Jesus.

This study also recognizes that no comprehensive christological portrait may be sketched on the basis of the titles. Within the Christian
tradition titles are always embedded within other literary forms: creeds,
hymns, confessions, parables, sayings, Gospels. The characterizations
of Jesus offered by the New Testament are ultimately narrative portraits
composed of various literary elements and delicate narrative transactions. Titles prove to be one element in complex patterns of narrative
characterization.[43]

---

42. M.A. Tolbert, *Sowing the Gospel: Mark's World in Literary-Historical Perspective* (Minneapolis: Fortress Press, 1989), pp. 122-23 n. 59.

43. This study of the titles is part of a much larger christological investigation.
See Edwin K. Broadhead, *Teaching with Authority: Miracles and Christology in
the Gospel of Mark* (JSNTSup, 74; Sheffield: JSOT Press, 1992); *idem, Prophet,
Son, Messiah: Narrative Form and Function in Mark 14–16* (JSNTSup, 97;
Sheffield: JSOT Press, 1994).

The investigation that follows recognizes that titles draw upon and reflect numerous levels of influence. The impact of concepts from the history of religions cannot be ignored. The activity and language of Jesus stands as the formative factor behind the early Christian movement. The practice and thought of early Christian groups remains decisive. The Evangelists shaped the christological material in various ways. As a consequence, there is no monolithic pattern of development behind the titles. The process of development varies for each term, and it is unclear for most of the titles. This investigation does not preclude interest in these various lines of development.

Nonetheless, this study insists that the first and foremost role of the titles is as narrative elements operating within a larger pattern of characterization. While external factors remain relevant, the titles receive their most decisive imprint from the literary strategy and the literary world which host them. In this sense the titles may be viewed as literary constructs shaped by the operations of their host.[44] Consequently the search for a Titular Christology denotes a stream of narrative presentation which constructs and employs various titles and images in the naming of Jesus. The outcome of such a process is not a systematic Christology, but a narrative presentation or performance. Such performances are typically noted more for their rhetorical impact than for their rational coherence. To describe the Gospels as narrative christological performances does not, however, imply they have no focus or claim. A significant part of the process of naming Jesus is the setting forth of the kerygmatic claims which surround his character and mission.

Because titles will be defined primarily in terms of their narrative foreground rather than their historical background, a number of unexpected images will present themselves for consideration. These have often been overlooked because they have no real background in the

---

44. This formalist analysis should not be confused with attempts to unveil 'Mark's literary contribution', for it says nothing about Mark. Formalism wholly avoids the 'intentional fallacy' which credits literary patterns to authorial intent. As far as possible formalism also avoids the 'affective fallacy'—the view which evaluates a work by its effect on the reader. In the analysis which follows, all intentionality is seen as inherent in the formal structures and strategies of the narrative. In the view of formalism the text ultimately provides a performance or presentation which need not be explained through external factors, though such factors obviously exist.

history of religions or no subsequent development in the early Church. Their role as narrative names for Jesus, however, will be clear.

This analysis will provide a formalist description of the narrative titles set against a *traditionsgeschichtliche* (history of traditions) context. Through this approach the uniqueness of the title or its dependence upon prior tradition will come into view. Each investigation will provide a broad sketch of the historical background of the title. Attention will then be given to the foreground of the title as it operates within the Gospel of Mark. This formalist analysis will note the distribution of the term through the Gospel and the patterns of association established around the title. The level of confirmation offered by the narrative will be analyzed. Attention will then be given to the development of the term within the larger literary strategy and to the effect of this strategy upon the christological presentation. A concluding statement will focus the formal operation of the title within the characterization of Jesus, particularly in light of other uses of this tradition. In order to demonstrate the distinction between the historical background of a title and its literary foreground, the initial investigation will analyze a title which has been assigned no real background—Jesus the Nazarene.

Chapter 2

JESUS THE NAZARENE

But he said to them, 'Do not be afraid. You are seeking Jesus the Nazarene...' (Mk 16.6).

The image of Jesus as a Nazarene may be used to demonstrate the literary impact of titles. Because the Nazarene title has no historical tradition and little redactional value, it provides an ideal test case through which to establish a wider model of analysis. By using a rather vacant image to demonstrate the literary role of titles, a model may be established by which to investigate more difficult cases—Son of God, Son of Man, Messiah.[1] This investigation will suggest that the narrative construction of the Nazarene imagery is paradigmatic of a larger literary and christological strategy which guides the Gospel of Mark.

The Historical Background

The Nazarene imagery has no historical background as a messianic title or image. The village of Nazareth is not mentioned in the Old Testament, in Josephus, or in rabbinical literature.[2] Thus, the use of the

---

1. The absence of historical background or clear redactional interest does not create the primary literary value of this title. The primary function of this title originates in the strategic world of the text. The relative isolation and simplicity of the Nazarene imagery brings its literary function into stark focus.

2. Luke has taken over the term Ναζαρηνός from Mk 1.24 (Lk. 4.34) and from his special material (Lk. 24.19), but otherwise prefers Ναζωραῖος. Matthew prefers Ναζωραῖος, but equates this with Ναζαρηνός. The New Testament usage obviously equates both Ναζαρηνός and Ναζωραῖος with the village of Nazareth, though the connection of Ναζωραῖος to Ναζαρετ is difficult to establish (see the argument of H.H. Schaeder, 'Ναζαρηνός, Ναζωραῖος', *TDNT*, IV, pp. 874-79). Mt. 26.71 substitutes Ναζωραῖος for Ναζαρηνός of Mk 14.67, demonstrating that Matthew sees both in connection with Nazareth. Mt. 2.23 implies a connection between Ναζωραῖος and the Nazarite tradition, though no text can be cited for this prophecy.

Nazarene imagery draws upon no historical or symbolic background. It emerges in the Gospel of Mark as a geographical designation which helps to clarify which Jesus is meant. Consequently, whatever impact the Nazarene imagery attains is due wholly to the literary framework within which it operates.

The Literary Foreground

While the description of Jesus as a Nazarene belies no prior history or symbolism, the Gospel of Mark makes significant use of this term. The following work will investigate the presence of the Nazarene imagery in the Gospel of Mark, then give attention to its role within the wider narrative. Subsequently the effect of this imagery upon the christological strategy will be considered.

Distribution

The Nazarene title or imagery appears only five times in the Gospel of Mark. In Mk 1.9 the term is used to describe Jesus' place of origin. In 1.24 Jesus is addressed as the Nazarene by an unclean spirit. Bartimaeus hears in 10.47 that Jesus the Nazarene is passing by. The servant of the high priest accuses Peter of association with the Nazarene (14.67). The messenger at the tomb refers to Jesus as the Nazarene (16.6). The sparse use of this imagery and its seeming unimportance prove misleading. Within the narrative world of the Gospel of Mark the Nazarene imagery is associated with key christological images.

Association

Although the Nazarene terminology is infrequent in the Gospel of Mark, the narrative role of this imagery is significant. Key associations are generated around each use of this term.

The first use of the Nazarene imagery appears in a non-titular form in Mk 1.9. Apart from the opening inscription, the first description of

The consecration of Jesus from the womb may suggest this connection, though Jesus hardly fulfilled the three major requirements for a Nazirite vow: abstention from wine, no contact with the dead, no cutting of the hair. The term was later applied to Christians and may point to a Jewish Christian group around Pella. Eduard Schweizer, '"Er wird Nazoräer heissen" (zu Mc 1.24; Mt 2.23)', in W. Eltester (ed.), *Judentum, Urchristentum, Kirche* (Festschrift J. Jeremias; Berlin: Alfred Töpelmann, 1964), pp. 90-93, argues that Ναζιραῖος and ἅγιος θεοῦ are variants of translation in the Septuagint (Judg. 13.7; 16.17).

Jesus tells of one 'from Nazareth of Galilee'. Several images are attached to this initial use: the baptism by John, the opening of the heavens, the descent of the Spirit. Most significantly, a divine voice declares 'You are my son, the Beloved One. In you I am well pleased' (1.11). Put in place even before the beginning of his ministry, the Nazarene imagery belongs to the initial portrait of Jesus as the Son of God.

The second use of the Nazarene image belongs to the initial day of Jesus' ministry (1.21-38). Both the geographical and the ideological setting prove significant. Geographically, Jesus opens his ministry in the synagogues of Galilee (1.39), specifically in Capernaum (1.21). Two images define the ideological context of this activity: teaching and authority. The teaching activity of Jesus provides the basic element in his ministry in Galilee (1.21): the people are amazed at the power displayed in his teaching (1.22). The summary description of Jesus' ministry in 1.22 is followed by a graphic exorcism in 1.23-28. The language of the story is violent: crying out (ἀνέκραζεν), destroying (ἀπολέσαι), warning (ἐπιτίμησιν), muzzling (φιμώθητι), tearing (σπαράξαν), making a loud noise (φωνῆσαν φωνῇμεγάλῃ). The broken grammar of the demon mimics the violence of his spirit: 'what to you and to me Jesus Nazarene?' The response of the people is amazement (1.27) and acclamation (1.28).

Mark 1.21-28 is thus built around elements typical of Hellenistic miracle stories.[3] Because of these similarities, many see here the presentation of Jesus as a Hellenistic divine man, or *theios anēr*. Jesus is proclaimed in Capernaum as 'the Holy One of God'[4] who has authority over unclean spirits. One element transforms the scene and distinguishes it from bare presentations of divine wonder: this healing is understood as indicative of Jesus' *teaching*. Consequently the christological focus of the story falls not on bare power, but on the authority of Jesus' message. Thus, the exorcism in 1.23-28 does not stand alone, but provides a clear demonstration of the authority present in Jesus' teaching (1.22).

---

3. The struggle with the demon, the recognition/naming of the opponent, the command to silence, the violent departure are typical elements. The use of πνεῦμα ἀκάθαρτον is frequent in Hellenistic Judaism.

4. The titular ὁ ἅγιος τοῦ θεοῦ, apparently deriving from a word-play on ναζιραῖος θεοῦ carries implications of a charismatic wonder worker. See Schweizer, 'Nazoräer'.

To this stark image is attached the Nazarene connection. Three levels of christological acclamation are present in this story. (1) 'We know who you are', cry the demons. To the unclean spirits, the Nazarene is the Holy One of God whom they must obey. (2) To the people, he is the one who 'teaches them as one having authority'. (3) The third level of acclamation belongs to the level of the reader, who is confronted with an open symbol; the deeper sense of the Nazarene title will be clarified only through the full impact of the narrative.

Thirdly, the Nazarene title is found in the healing scene of Mk 10.46-52. Bartimaeus has heard that the one passing by is 'Jesus the Nazarene'. Through the expectation and insistence of the blind beggar, various images are attached to the Nazarene title. (1) The Nazarene title connotes power. In the larger narrative this expectation is drawn from the images of authority presented in Mk 1.9 and 1.24. Within the story the recognition of the Nazarene produces a clear expectation of power. This expectation is clarified in the request of Bartimaeus 'that I might see again' (10.51). (2) Mark 10.46-52 also associates the power of Jesus with his role as teacher. The request for healing is addressed to Jesus as the Teacher—ῥαββουνί ἵνα ἀναβλέψω (10.51). (3) Jesus is further named as Son of David, a royal messianic title associated with Israel's hopes. This connection takes up and extends the imagery of the baptismal scene. (4) The authority of Jesus is specified in a new direction by Bartimaeus. The recognition of Jesus and his authority evokes from Bartimaeus a plea for mercy (ἐλέησον με in 10.47, 48). Thus, the authority of Jesus is expressed as mercy which is able to save (10.52). (5) Also associated with the Nazarene title is the task of discipleship. Following his confrontation with the Nazarene, Bartimaeus 'follows him in the way'. The connection of his way to the passion story lies close at hand.

Thus, the use of the Nazarene title in Mk 10.47 takes up prior connections and further extends the scope of the title. Jesus the Nazarene carries authority to heal and to save. This authority is connected to Jesus' identity as the Teacher and as Son of David. This power expresses itself in terms of mercy and discipleship. Consequently the Nazarene imagery takes on a rich variety of narrative connections.

The fourth use of the term is found in the context of Jesus' trial in Mk 14.67. This use of the Nazarene title conveys the conflict and abandonment which surround the ministry of Jesus. Here the Nazarene has been arrested by religious leaders (14.53). His trial subjects him to false witnesses (14.56-59), the charge of blasphemy (14.63-64) and a death sentence (14.64). As a result of this trial Jesus is spit upon, beaten, mocked (14.65). More significantly, Jesus is abandoned by his own. He has been betrayed by one of the Twelve (14.18-20, 43-44). He has been abandoned by his followers (14.50). Now he is denied three times by Peter (14.66-72). This scene of torture, abandonment and rejection is tied specifically to the Nazarene imagery: the servant of the high priest insists 'You were with Jesus the Nazarene'.

The final use of the Nazarene imagery occurs outside the ministry of Jesus in the resurrection promise of Mk 16.1-8. 'You are seeking Jesus the Nazarene', says the messenger to the women at the tomb. Here the Nazarene title is connected to the image of Jesus as the Crucified One who has been raised to go before his followers into Galilee (16.6-7).

Confirmation
The narrative assumes the validity of the Nazarene imagery. The terminology is used by a mixed host: by the narrator (1.9), by unclean spirits (1.24), by the people (10.47), by a servant of the high priest (14.67), by the messenger at the tomb (16.6). The title and its images are neither perjoritive nor laudatory. The use of the term is never debated, nor is any apology offered in its support. Like the name Jesus, the Nazarene imagery belongs inherently to the characterization of Jesus.

Development
The obscure Nazarene title is developed through two strategic patterns. The content of the Nazarene imagery is gained through its connection with various images of Jesus. The value of the Nazarene imagery is created through the vital position it occupies in the plot line of the Gospel of Mark.

The various images connected to the Nazarene title generate its *content*. In Mk 1.9 the Nazarene imagery is associated with the coming of the Spirit, with the sign and voice from heaven, and with the declaration that Jesus is the Son of God.

In Mk 1.24 the Nazarene imagery is associated with a graphic christological portrait. Jesus is the *Wundermann* (miracle worker), the Holy One who works miracles in the name of God. This display of authority is linked to the teaching ministry of Jesus (1.22). The power of the miracle worker is without parallel (1.22, 27), and the report of his wonders spreads far and wide (1.28). Thus, the Nazarene imagery has a

primary association with Jesus' authoritative teaching and his spectac-
ular miracle activity.

In Mk 10.47, the Nazarene title is associated with a host of images.
Jesus the Nazarene is the Teacher and the Son of David. An expectation
of creative power and authority marks his presence. The use of this
authority is characterized by healing, by mercy, by salvation. Discipleship belongs to the way of the Nazarene.

A different imagery is associated with the Nazarene title in Mk
14.67. In contrast to the power and amazement of Capernaum, this
scene is marked by helplessness and rejection. Jesus is under the control of secular authorities. He stands under the condemnation of religious leaders. He has been betrayed by one of his own followers and
denied three times by Peter. Here the Nazarene title is filled out by
images of Jesus as a rejected servant of God.

Further elements are ascribed to the Nazarene title in Mk 16.6. Here
the image of the Nazarene is joined concretely to the destiny of Jesus as
the Crucified One. A new status is declared: 'He has been raised.' A
new destiny is given: 'He will go before you into Galilee.' In this
manner the Nazarene title inherits the full image of Jesus as the one
crucified who has been raised to lead his community into the future.

The accumulation of these various connections proves significant.
What began as an empty sign, void of all historical reference and intrinsic symbolic value, has been transformed into a deeply etched image of
Jesus. The Nazarene imagery now conveys a richly textured portrait.
The Nazarene is the Beloved Son of God. He is the wondrous miracle
worker whose teaching bears unparalleled authority. He is the Teacher
and Son of David whose power is expressed in saving mercy. At the
same time the Nazarene is the servant of God whose way is marked by
rejection, abuse and abandonment. Ultimately Jesus the Nazarene is the
Crucified One who has been raised by God as the shepherd of the new
community (14.27-28; 16.1-8). Through its connection to these various literary sites the Nazarene title is transformed into a rich, deeply
nuanced image of Jesus.

The *value* of the Nazarene imagery is created through the vital position it occupies in the plot line of the Gospel of Mark. Nazarene
imagery accompanies the baptism of Jesus and his designation as the
Son of God who bears the Spirit. The Nazarene title appears on the first
day of Jesus' activity and becomes part of a larger paradigm of Jesus'
ministry. Prior to his entry into Jerusalem the powerful mercy of the

Nazarene is demonstrated. The Nazarene title appears on the eve of Jesus' passion and embodies the hostility and rejection which lead to his death. The Nazarene title is employed in the door of the empty tomb to speak of the paradoxical destiny of Jesus: he is at once the Crucified One and the one who goes before. This location of the Nazarene title at vital junctures of Jesus' story generates crucial narrative significance.

Three literary traits combine to create this significance: primacy, repetition, triadic structure. The Gospel of Mark tends to put 'up front' the issues that matter, then to develop them through patterns of repetition, particularly in groups of three. All of these strategies are applied to the Nazarene imagery.

The Gospel of Mark creates a primacy effect for its central themes. These concerns are focused early in the narrative, then echoed through subsequent development. Mark 1.1-20, for example, establishes the priority of the following themes: the gospel, Christology, fulfillment of Scripture, the Spirit, the divine calling of Jesus, resistance to evil, service to others, Galilee, the preaching mission, the kingdom, repentance, faith. A vital part of this initial image is the designation of Jesus as the Nazarene (1.9).

In a similar manner the sabbath at Capernaum (1.21-39) provides a model for Jesus' larger ministry. His teaching with authority is set over against the teaching of the scribes, thus providing the conditions for conflict. The authority of his teaching is demonstrated through three miracle scenes (1.23-28, 29-31, 32-34). These scenes provide a model for Jesus' interaction with the synagogue and his sabbath controversies. On the first day of his ministry, women and service are emphasized (1.29-31). The central role of Simon is focused (1.29, 36). Demons are forbidden to make his identity known, initiating a secrecy motif (1.34). The role of the crowd is set forth (1.22, 27-28, 32-33, 37). The first report of Jesus' activity spreads throughout Galilee (1.28). Jesus' itinerant preaching ministry is begun (1.38-39). Consequently the first day of Jesus' ministry provides a paradigm for the entirety of his work. The designation of Jesus as the Nazarene belongs to this paradigm.

Acting as an overture, the opening scenes of this Gospel establish the central themes and the primary model for Jesus' ministry. These initial images cast a long and distinct shadow across the larger narrative. The use of the Nazarene image in Mk 1.9 and 1.24 participates in this primacy effect.

The Gospel of Mark repeats crucial events, typically in triads. The most prominent examples of this strategy are the passion predictions (8.31; 9.31; 10.32-34), three denials by Peter (14.66-72), three scenes of prayer in Gethsemene (14.32-42), three external witnesses (1.10-11; 9.7; 16.5-7). The strategy behind the Nazarene title conforms to this pattern. The fivefold use of the image reinforces the initial impact. In addition, the use of the image occurs in three distinct settings: the beginning of Jesus' ministry (1.9, 24), in the context of the passion (10.47; 14.67), on the day of the resurrection (16.6). Thus, the Nazarene imagery belongs to the larger pattern of theme and reinforcement typical of the Gospel of Mark. Through this strategy the Nazarene imagery inhabits the major regions of Jesus' story.

In addition to this reinforcing effect, the Gospel of Mark employs triadic repetition of a theme to generate variation and intensification. Through the progression of the triad different aspects of the theme tend to come to light. In addition, the reader comes to expect the climax of the theme in the third appearance.[5] The three settings of the Nazarene imagery also conform to this strategy. Each use contributes a new perspective, and the final use of the imagery proves climactic.

Effect

This literary conspiracy generates a decisive characterization of Jesus. Both the content and the design of this Christology prove significant.

Various *contents* are joined around the Nazarene title. These images provide a character study marked by contrast and complexity. Jesus the Nazarene is the Son of God, the Holy One who silences the shrieks of demons, the Teacher whose authority exceeds that of the scribes, the Son of David in mercy and power. These images of power are countered by stark images of suffering: Jesus the Nazarene is arrested, accused, beaten, betrayed, abandoned. This paradox of suffering and glory is played out in the final image of Jesus: he is at once the Crucified One whose way ended in Jerusalem and the one who has been raised to go before them into Galilee. Thus, a number of contrasting images cohere around the image of the Nazarene, creating a Christology which is not monolithic, but polyvalent and paradoxical.

---

5.   On the narrative role of triads, see D. Rhoads and D. Michie, *Mark as Story: An Introduction to the Narrative of a Gospel* (Philadelphia: Fortress Press, 1982), pp. 54-55.

The *design* of this Christology is unique. Through this strategy the polyvalent imagery of the Nazarene is gathered into a single focal stream. To accomplish this Mk 16.6 links a seldom-used image (Jesus the Nazarene) to an unparalleled title (the Crucified One).[6] Here, at the climax of the narrative, Jesus is identified for the first and only time by the title which interprets all titles. While the prism of his story has many facets and angles, it has but one focal point. In this way the varied imagery of Jesus the Nazarene is gathered under the hermeneutic of the cross. At the same time the image of the cross is filled out by the full story of Jesus' life and ministry.

Thus, a complex narrative strategy operates upon the Nazarene terminology to effect a sharp christological image. Through this strategy contrasting views of Jesus are joined in a paradoxical, yet coherent, focus. Consequently the risen Lord who will appear to his followers in Galilee is no mystical projection of human need and desire. He is, instead, the one crucified in scandalous shame. This Crucified One is no empty symbol, no hollow metaphor in the transaction of atonement. The Crucified One is none other than Jesus, who lived the concrete and complex life of the Nazarene.

The christological design demonstrated around the Nazarene image is indicative of the larger world of the Gospel of Mark. This is a Gospel inhabited by complexity and contradiction. Many images of Jesus are sketched across the pages of this story,[7] and the paradoxical nature of this portrait is evident. Jesus is, in the words of Werner Kelber, a character

> fraught with ambiguity and paradox. Jesus announces the Kingdom but opts for the cross; he is King of the Jews but condemned by the Jewish establishment; he asks for followers but speaks in riddles; he is identified

6. 'You are seeking Jesus the Nazarene, the Crucified One', says the messenger. The resurrection of Jesus and his absence are described as activities of Jesus; hence the verbal ἠγέρθη, and οὐκ ἔστιν ὧδε. In contrast the cross belongs to the very identity of Jesus; hence the substantive τὸν ἐσταυρωμένον.

7. He is the mighty preacher/teacher, the powerful healer, the exorcist without equal, the priestly servant of God. Jesus is the caller of disciples, the ruler over chaos, the epiphany of God's power and presence, God's compassionate shepherd. Jesus is the prophet of old who founds the new community of faith. He is the giver of life who journeys to his death in Jerusalem. Various titles attest to his character: he is Jesus the Nazarene, the Holy One of God, the Messiah. He is the Teacher. He is the son—Son of God, Son of Man, Son of David. Jesus is the shepherd who will be struck down, then raised up. He is the Crucified One.

as Nazarene but rejected in Nazareth; he makes public announcements but also hides behind a screen of secrecy; he saves others but not himself; he promises return but has not returned; he performs miracles but suffers a non-miraculous death; he is appointed by God in power but dies abandoned by God in powerlessness; he dies but rises from death. His beginning is nebulous and his future status is indefinite, and at the moment of Messianic disclosure he still speaks enigmatically of himself in the third person... If there is one single feature which characterizes the Markan Jesus it is contradiction or paradox.[8]

Recent Markan scholarship has addressed this paradox through two major models. Theodore Weeden has proposed a model of conflict.[9] For Weeden the first half of the Gospel reports the false 'divine man' Christology of the disciples. The second half of the Gospel obliterates this false Christology of power and wonder through a concerted focus on the cross. Weeden's thesis provides a rather dramatic route to a conclusion first stated by Martin Kähler: the Gospels are passion narratives with extensive introductions.[10]

A second model sees in the Gospel of Mark a corrective synthesis which combines two major traditions about Jesus.[11] These proposals

---

8.   Werner Kelber, 'From Passion Narrative to Gospel', in *idem* (ed.), *The Passion in Mark: Studies on Mark 14–16* (Philadelphia: Fortress Press, 1976), pp. 153-80 (179).

9.   Weeden, *Traditions in Conflict*.

10.   Kähler, *So-Called Historical Jesus*.

11.   For examples of corrective Christology see Johannes Schreiber, 'Die Christologie des Markusevangeliums', *ZTK* 58 (1961), 154-83 (pp. 158-59); Eduard Schweizer, *The Good News According to Mark* (Atlanta: John Knox Press, 1970), pp. 380-86; Ulrich Luz, 'Das Geheimnismotiv und die markinische Christologie', *ZNW* 56 (1965), pp. 9-30 (28-30); Leander Keck, 'Mark 3.7-12 and Mark's Christology', *JBL* 84 (1965), pp. 341-48; Paul Achtemeier, 'Origin and Function of the Pre-Marcan Miracle Catenae', *JBL* 91 (1972), pp. 198-221; Ludger Schenke, *Die Wundererzählungen des Markusevangeliums* (Stuttgart: Katholisches Bibelwerk, 1974); pp. 373-417, but especially pp. 390-95; Karl Kertelge, *Die Wunder Jesu im Markusevangelium: Eine redaktionsgeschichtliche Untersuchung* (SANT, 23; Munich: Kösel, 1970), pp. 208-10; Dietrich-Alex Koch, *Die Bedeutung der Wundererzählungen für die Christologie des Markusevangelium* (Berlin: W. de Gruyter, 1975), pp. 180-93; Gottfried Schille, *Die urchristliche Wundertradition: Ein Beitrag zur Frage nach dem irdischen Jesus* (Stuttgart: Calwer Verlag, 1967); Weeden, *Traditions in Conflict*, pp. 159-68; Perrin, 'Towards an Interpretation', p. 38; Achtemeier, *Mark*, pp. 41-50, but especially pp. 45-48; Petersen, *Literary Criticism for New Testament Critics*, pp. 60-68, especially p. 63; Kelber, *The*

build upon a presumption that the Gospels' material divides conceptually into two distinct parts: power Christology versus passion Christology. Throughout this model Mark is seen as one who consciously employed passion Christology to realign other traditions about Jesus.

My own work on the literary structure and strategy of the Gospel of Mark confirms a different model: the Gospel of Mark is a unified literary piece, and its christological imagery is marked by paradoxical coherence.[12] The pattern of this Gospel is not a *reflexive* strategy in which the passion story recasts the entire Gospel in its image (thus Kähler and a host of followers). Neither is this Gospel controlled by a *repressive* pattern in which the passion story subsumes all other traditions. Instead, the Gospel of Mark employs a *reciprocal* strategy of characterization. The intricate and paradoxical image of Jesus emerges from a complex strategy of reciprocity and reinterpretation. Through a process of mutual engagement the death story partakes of the wider interpretive world of the narrative. Through this intratextual process the passion account both shapes and is shaped by the larger portrait of Jesus. All lines of characterization remain effective, with none consumed and none unchanged.

Nowhere is this strategy more evident than in Mk 16.1-8. The naming of Jesus by an external witness as the Crucified One provides the decisive title which comprehends the scattered images of Jesus, yet this title threatens to become a term without definition and content. The scrolls of Jewish and Roman history are filled with crucified ones, and two others were crucified with Jesus. Read in isolation the title tends to be an empty symbol.

The designation of Jesus as the Crucified One in Mk 16.6 gains interpretive depth only through the wider transactions of the narrative. This singular image has been linked through the Nazarene title to the larger story of Jesus. The climactic focus on the Crucified One is thus undergirded by the whole energy of the narrative and by its intricate, paradoxical portrait of Jesus. Jesus' suffering and death culminates the story

---

Kingdom in Mark, pp. 21-22, 62-65, 84-85, 132-37, 138-47; Etienne Trocmé, *The Formation of the Gospel According to Mark* (London: SPCK, 1975 [1963]); Burton Mack, *Mark and Christian Origins: A Myth of Innocence* (Philadelphia: Fortress Press, 1988).

12. See Broadhead, *Teaching with Authority*; and *Prophet, Son, Messiah*. See also the literature listed in these works.

of his life; the whole of his life story undergirds his final destiny. He is Jesus the Nazarene, the Crucified One.[13]

Conclusion

This study begins with a term that is inherently empty and ambiguous in order to focus the role of titles in the Gospel of Mark. The value of this title cannot be demonstrated from any historical background, any connection to Jesus or the early Church, nor any redactional interests of an author. The significance of the Nazarene title is an acquired significance drawn from the literary system in which it circulates. Through association with vital images of Jesus and through strategic placement at key junctures of Jesus' story the Nazarene title is transformed into a complex christological image. At the end of the story it is joined to the most decisive image of the narrative: the Crucified One who goes before the community is none other than Jesus, the Nazarene. In the Gospel of Mark this use of the Nazarene imagery is paradigmatic for a larger christological strategy of reciprocity and reinterpretation.

A fruitful field of research lies before us. The titles are not primarily historical or redactional signposts, nor are they simply theological collection points. Like the Nazarene imagery, all titles must be seen as literary elements participating in particular narrative worlds and narrative strategies. This formalist approach does not reduce the significance of such images nor deny their historical development; it promises rather to bring to light their particular narrative and kerygmatic identity. This study will demonstrate that titles such as the Nazarene play a crucial role as building blocks in the kerygma, the *story* of Jesus the Christ.

---

13. On the narrative impact of the title Crucified One see Chapter 17.

Chapter 3

PROPHET

> And Jesus said to them, 'A prophet is not without honor except in his
> home town and among his own people and in his own house' (Mk 6.4).

Of all the titles applied to Jesus, the image of the prophet has the most
extensive historical background. In addition, the early Church use of
this title is among the most enigmatic. Both the historical development
and the literary function of this title are noteworthy.

The Historical Background

Christological use of the prophet title draws indirectly upon a wide and
varied background in the history of religions. More direct influence
may be seen in particular aspects of Jewish prophetic tradition.

Greco-Roman Prophecy

Prophecy served as a typical element in the Greco-Roman world: 'The
mantic arts, ranging from technical divination to inspired divination,
were an integral feature of the social and religious life of the Greeks
during the entire Greco-Roman period.'[1] Prophetic activity was not
limited to times of social or personal distress, but belonged to the whole
range of socio-religious existence. All matters of life were subjected to
oracular inquiry.[2]

The role of prophecy in the mystery cults was quite different. Here
states of ecstasy were equated with divine inspiration. The prophet was
understood as a passive instrument for divine speech, and this was confirmed through the state of possession.[3] Greek oracles tended to be

---

1. David E. Aune, *Prophecy in Early Christianity and the Ancient Mediterranean World* (Grand Rapids: Eerdmans, 1983), p. 47.
2. Aune, *Prophecy*, p. 47.
3. Aune, *Prophecy*, pp. 47-48.

poetic in form and enigmatic in content.[4] The oracle was typically given in response to an inquiry, and it took various forms.[5]

Prophecy in Ancient Israel

The distinct understanding of prophecy which arose in ancient Israel and extended into early Judaism proves more influential for prophetic forms of Christology. A variety of terms and images were employed. Eventually the terms for a 'seer' (*hozeh, ro'eh*) were replaced with *nabi'*. Although the Septuagint gathered all prophetic images under the single term προφήτης, prophecy in ancient Israel was a diverse phenomenon.

Various forms of divination were practiced in ancient Israel. While this activity was largely condemned,[6] some forms of divination were tolerated or approved. Among these were the interpretation of dreams (Gen. 20.3, 6-7; 28.12-15; 31.10-13; 37.5-11; Judg. 7.13-14; 1 Kgs 3.5-15); sacred lot—especially the Urim and Thummin (Deut. 33.8; Num. 27.21); the priest's ephod (1 Sam. 23.6, 9; 30.7); and consultation with small, portable images known as teraphim (Ezek. 21.21; Zech. 10.2).

The mainstream of Israelite prophecy followed a different direction. Acceptable prophetic activity took varied, sometimes conflicting forms of expression.

Shamanistic prophets appeared from the eleventh century BCE in figures such as Samuel, Elijah, Elisha. These early figures combined the roles of holy man, sage, miracle worker, soothsayer (1 Sam. 9; 1 Kgs 17; 2 Kgs 1.2-17; 6.1-7, 8-10; 13.14-21; 20.1-11). They were connected with sacred places and ritual (1 Sam. 7.17; 9.11-14; 10.1-5), serving at times as both priest and prophet (1 Sam. 2.18-20; 3.1, 19-20). These itinerant leaders presided over prophetic guilds (1 Sam. 19.20, 24; 2 Kgs 4.38; 6.22) and appeared in distinct clothing associated with their function (2 Kgs 1.8; Zech. 13.4).[7]

Cult and Temple prophets arose in relation to Judah and the Temple cult at Jerusalem. This cultic framework may be seen at work in Amos (Amos 7.10-13), Isaiah (Isa. 6.1-13), Jeremiah (Jer. 26.2, 7; 27.16-22;

---

4.   Aune, *Prophecy*, pp. 50-52.
5.   Aune, *Prophecy*, pp. 54-80.
6.   Lev. 19.26; Deut. 18.10; 1 Sam. 15.23; 28.2; 2 Kgs 17.17; 21.6; Isa. 3.2; Jer. 27.7; 29.8; Ezek. 13.6, 9; 22.28; Mic. 3.11; Zech. 10.2.
7.   Aune, *Prophecy*, p. 84.

28.1, 5), Haggai and Zechariah (Ezra 5.1-2). Liturgical form survives in the work of such classical prophets as Joel, Nahum, Habakkuk, Zephaniah. Even for non-cultic prophets like Jeremiah, the Temple provided a logical focus for prophetic activity (Jer. 10).[8]

Court prophets also functioned in Israel. While the Baal prophets who served Ahab and Jezebel are condemned (1 Kgs 18.19; see 2 Kgs 3.13), prophets also ministered to the kings of Israel. Gad is the king's seer (2 Sam. 4.11; 1 Chron. 21.9; 2 Chron. 29.25). Asaph, Heman and Jeduthun are seers for King David (1 Chron. 25.5; 2 Chron. 35.15). Nathan seems to serve as the court prophet of David (2 Sam. 7.14-17; 12.1-17; 1 Kgs 1.8, 10, 22-37).[9]

The Assyrian threat saw the development of isolated prophetic figures in the eighth century BCE. Amos and Hosea embodied this function in Israel, while Micah and Isaiah held this role in Judah. Acting as reformers independent of kings and priests, these figures called Israel back to the ancient covenant and its theocratic ideals. This activity frequently placed the independent prophets in conflict with the king and his prophets, and the distinction between true and false prophets became an important issue.[10]

Israelite prophecy is known as a written phenomenon beginning from the eighth century BCE. Writing of prophecy emerged in the political crises which surrounded and threatened Israel in this period. This writing seeks to authenticate prophecies in view of the future time when these predictions come to pass. Pre-exilic collections generally exhibit a complex, layered compositional identity. Deutero-prophetic writings arise in the postexilic period and are inserted into or appended to earlier prophetic works.[11]

Prophecy in Early Judaism
More distinct antecedants to prophetic Christology emerge from early Judaism. Aune divides the prophetic activity of this period into four

---

8. Aune, *Prophecy*, p. 84.

9. Aune, *Prophecy*, pp. 84-85.

10. Aune, *Prophecy*, pp. 85-88. On the distinction of true and false prophets, see J.L. Crenshaw, *Prophetic Conflict: Its Effect upon Israelite Religion* (Berlin: W. de Gruyter, 1971); J. Blenkinsopp, *Prophecy and Canon: A Contribution to the Study of Jewish Origin* (Notre Dame: University of Notre Dame Press, 1977); S.J. DeVries, *Prophet against Prophet: The Role of the Micaiah Narrative (1 Kings 22) in the Development of Early Prophetic Tradition* (Grand Rapids: Eerdmans, 1978).

11. Aune, *Prophecy*, p. 101.

types: apocalyptic, eschatological, clerical, sapiential.[12]

First, David Aune describes the apocalyptic line as

> ...a form of revelatory literature in which the author narrates both the
> visions he has purportedly experienced and their meaning, usually
> elicited through a dialogue between the seer and an interpreting angel.
> The substance of these revelatory visions is the imminent intervention of
> God into human affairs to bring the present evil world system to an end
> and to replace it with an ideal one. This transformation is accompanied
> by the punishment of the wicked and the reward of the righteous.[13]

J.J. Collins offers a more formal definition of apocalypse as a literary
genre. An apocalypse is defined as

> a genre of revelatory literature with a narrative framework, in which a
> revelation is mediated by an otherworldly being to a human recipient,
> disclosing a transcendent reality which is both temporal, insofar as it
> envisages eschatological salvation, and spatial, insofar as it involves
> another, supernatural world.[14]

Apocalyptic literature generally invoked the name of an ancient authority to legitimate its message. The primary social context of this
literature was intramural: the prophetic-eschatological outlook of apocalyptic writers was set over against a priestly-theocratic perspective
within postexilic Judaism. While it is not identical to the classic prophecy of Israel, continuity exists between apocalyptic literature and the
earlier prophets.[15] Aune concludes that 'Apocalyptic literature is historically and genetically derived from the various revelatory media of
ancient Israel, of which classical prophecy was the most important
exemplar'.[16]

Secondly, a non-eschatological clerical prophecy also exists in early
Judaism.[17] The association of prophet and priest is found in the early
stages of Israelite prophecy, particularly in association with the Urim
and Thummin. The idea of levitical prophecy is seen in the Chronicler.
This connection may also be found in early Judaism. Philo knows this

---

12. Aune, *Prophecy*, pp. 106-107.

13. Aune, *Prophecy*, p. 108.

14. J.J. Collins, *The Apocalyptic Imagination: Introduction to the Jewish Matrix
of Christianity* (New York: Crossroad, 1989), p. 4.

15. Aune, *Prophecy*, pp. 109-14.

16. Aune, *Prophecy*, p. 114.

17. Aune, *Prophecy*, pp. 138-44.

association,[18] as does Josephus.[19] Josephus, himself a priest, describes his own work in prophetic images.[20] This priestly prophecy emerges at two places in the New Testament. The prophecy of John's birth comes to Zechariah in the midst of his priestly duties (Lk. 1.5-23). Caiaphas can prophesy that Jesus will die for the nation precisely from his position as high priest (Jn 11.49-52).

Thirdly, a different line of non-eschatological prophecy is found in the sapiential or Wisdom traditions.[21] Sapiential prophecy in Palestine belongs to the Hasidic tradition. In addition to this rabbinic prophecy, Josephus cites examples of Essene prophecy. The clearest linkage of Wisdom and prophecy in the Diaspora is found in Philo of Alexandria (e.g. *Vit. Mos.* 2.163, 188).

The most significant antecedants to prophetic Christology lie in the expectations within early Judaism for an eschatological prophet.[22] This period was marked by a generalized perception that prophecy had ceased (Ps. 74.9; 1 Macc. 4.46; 9.27; 14.41), though various aspects of prophetic activity continued.[23] The expectation of a coming eschatological prophet found its focal point in various Old Testament figures: Moses, Elijah, Enoch, Ezra.

Deuteronomy 18.15 sponsors the hope for an eschatological prophet like Moses. At times the return of Moses himself is expected.[24] The unusual manner of Moses' death and burial (Deut. 34.5-6) allowed an association with Enoch and Elijah, who were translated into heaven. The prophecy in Deuteronomy 18 does not explicitly refer to an eschatological prophet, but rather to the succession of prophetic leadership. In a perceived absence of prophecy, this text could easily be seen as the promised renewal of prophecy. This expectation of renewal may take on eschatological aspects in the Servant of Yahweh figure from Deutero-Isaiah, though this is uncertain.[25] The Samaritan expectation of

18. *Praem. Poen.* 55-56; *Spec. Leg.* 192; *Vit. Mos.* 2.2, 187, 275.

19. *Ant.* 11.327-28; 10.79-80; 13.282-83, 299, 300; *War* 1.68-69, 169. See also J. Blenkinsopp, 'Prophecy and Priesthood in Josephus', *JJS* 25 (1974), pp. 239-62.

20. See, for example, *War* 3.351-54.

21. Aune, *Prophecy*, pp. 144-52.

22. Aune, *Prophecy*, pp. 121-38.

23. See Hahn, *Titles*, pp. 352-54; Aune, *Prophecy*, pp. 103-106.

24. See H.M. Teeple, *The Mosaic Eschatological Prophet* (JBLMS, 10; Philadelphia: Society of Biblical Literature, 1957).

25. Prophetic aspects of the Servant are emphasized by W. Zimmerli, 'παῖς θεοῦ', *TDNT*, V, pp. 654-77, especially pp. 659-73; Aage Bentzen, *King and*

the *Taheb*, the 'returning one', also exhibits links to Deut. 18.15 and to the return of Moses.[26]

The expected return of Elijah is wholly eschatological. This expectation is grounded in Mal. 3.1; 4.5-6: Elijah will come as the final prophet before the 'great and terrible day of the Lord comes' (Mal. 4.5). The expectation is confirmed by Jesus ben Sirach (Ecclus 48.10-11), by the New Testament (Mk 9.11-13), and by rabbinic sources.[27]

This generalized expectation of the renewal of prophecy became associated with the renewed activity of the Spirit and with the end time. These images merge in the prophecy of Joel 2.28-32: the last days will be marked by a renewal of the Spirit, by the distribution of prophetic gifts, and by eschatological woes.

Some expectation for the return of Enoch exists (*1 En.* 90.31), and two prophets are expected in some texts.[28] The expectation of Jeremiah's return is noted in Mt. 6.14.

The clearest and earliest application of Deut. 18.15 to the eschatological prophet comes from the Qumran literature of the first century BCE. 1QS 9.10-11 and 4QTestim 1-20 look for the prophet who will come. For the members of the Qumran community the Teacher of Righteousness was this eschatological Mosaic prophet.[29] This identification was accompanied by the self-understanding of the Qumran community as one endowed with the Spirit. The prophetic focus of the Teacher stood at the center of this community:

> The Teacher of Righteousness is a prophet of God. All the characteristic features of a prophet apply to him. Like the prophets he receives his instructions from the mouth of God. He has been selected by God to declare to the last generation the coming act of God. His word necessitates a decision on the part of those who hear it. Whoever does not carry

---

Messiah (Oxford: Basil Blackwell, rev. edn, 1970), pp. 48-72; Sigmund Mowinckel, *He That Cometh* (trans. G. Anderson; Oxford: Basil Blackwell, 1959 [1951]), pp. 187-257; Gerhard von Rad, *Old Testament Theology* (2 vols.; trans. D. Stalker; Edinburgh: Oliver & Boyd, 1965 [1960]), II, pp. 250-62.

26. Hahn, *Titles*, p. 359.

27. See Str-B, IV, pp. 779-98.

28. Enoch and Elijah are expected in *1 En.* 90.31 and the *Apocalypse of Elijah*. Moses and Elijah come in Mk 9.2-8 and in the midrash *Deut. R.* 3.10.1. Two witnesses are expected in Rev. 11.3-13.

29. See Aune, *Prophecy*, pp. 126, 132-35; Cullmann, *Christology*, pp. 19-21.

out the words of the Teacher, he is guilty and faces judgment. Whoever observes the word of the Teacher will also be saved from final judgment.[30]

Thus, the New Testament period is preceded by the expectation within early Judaism of a returning prophet who will renew the prophetic activity of the Spirit and prepare the way for the final acts of Yahweh. The bridge between this early Jewish expectation and the New Testament world of thought is found in a singular prophetic figure: John the Baptist.

The prophetic identity of the Baptist is never questioned in the New Testament, nor is the eschatological nature of his work challenged. The issue that remains open is the relation of this prophetic figure to the Old Testament, to Jesus and to the coming of God.

The Baptist is clearly 'a prophet'. Various aspects of his story place him in the line of prophetic figures from the Old Testament: (1) his clothing recalls that of the Old Testament prophets; (2) he is filled with the Spirit from his birth (Lk. 1.15); (3) a prophetic revelation formula is applied in Lk. 3.2: 'the word of the Lord came to John the son of Zechariah in the wilderness'; (4) the rebuke of Herod's immorality recalls the ancient prophets of Israel; (5) his call for repentance echoes the classic prophets; (6) John's message is addressed to all of Israel, not to a select band.[31]

More significantly, some accepted John as 'the Prophet'. While the mainstream of the New Testament tradition views John as the forerunner of Jesus the Messiah, echoes remain of some who saw in John the last messenger preparing the way before God's coming. To these John was not the forerunner of the messiah, but the forerunner of God. The words taken from Isa. 40.3—'Prepare the way of the Lord'—have their primary reference to Yahweh's coming (Mk 1.2-3; Mt. 3.1-6; Lk. 3.1-6; Jn 1.23). Similarly, Lk. 1.76 refers to John as God's forerunner. Luke 1.17 makes this position clear: John goes forth in the spirit and power of Elijah to prepare a people for God. Matthew 11.7-15 sees the Baptist as the returned Elijah, the final prophet who recapitulates all prophecy (Mt. 11.13). The stark denial of any identification with Elijah or the prophet in Jn 1.19-23, 25 provides clear evidence that some held this view of John.

---

30. Gert Jeremias, *Der Lehrer der Gerechtigkeit* (Göttingen: Vandenhoeck & Ruprecht, 1963), p. 141.

31. These traits are cited by Aune, *Prophecy*, p. 130.

In this role John the Baptist takes on messianic dimensions. Later followers of the Baptist clearly understood him as the Messiah.[32] Luke 3.15 knows that this view was already proposed in John's lifetime. For some, John was messianic: he was the last prophet, the one anointed with God's Spirit to usher in the final work of God. Oscar Cullmann concludes that

> According to the original conviction of the Baptist's disciples, then, John is actually the Prophet of the end time, whose function is sufficient in itself and requires no Messiah to come after him, since he himself prepares the way for God to establish his kingdom.[33]

The energy expended by the New Testament to suppress the messianic aura of John the Baptist testifies to the ongoing vitality of this position.[34] By the time of the Pseudo-Clementines (at the beginning of the second century CE), Jesus is understood as the true prophet and John as a false prophet.[35] This development also argues for the persistence of messianic views which saw in John the eschatological prophet whose ministry is the last act preceding the inbreak of God.

The image of the endtime prophet modeled in John the Baptist was seen in various other Jewish figures. Josephus notes a variety of messianic prophets in the first century; with the exception of John the Baptist, all come after the time of Jesus. A Samaritan arose in 35 CE claiming access to the Mosaic Temple vessels hidden on Gerazim. His movement was halted by Pontius Pilate (*Ant.* 18.85-89). Cuspius Fadus suppressed a messianic movement under Theudas, who promised to re-enact the crossing of the Jordan (*Ant.* 20.97-98; Acts 5.36). An Egyptian prophet promised to repeat the Jericho story at the walls of Jerusalem (*Ant.* 20.169-72). He was captured by Felix (52–60 CE), but escaped; Acts 21.38 expects his reappearance. A *sicarius* named Jonathan appeared in Cyrene and led a group of Jewish followers into the Libyan Pentapolis to view his miracle activity (*War.* 7.437-50). A similar messianic Jewish movement is known from Crete in the fifth

---

32. In the Pseudo-Clementines, see *Recg.* 1.60. The Mandean sect saw John as the true prophet over against Jesus as a false prophet. On this issue, see Cullmann, *Christology*, p. 27.

33. Cullmann, *Christology*, pp. 26-27.

34. See, for example, Mt. 11.11b; Jn 1.20; 3.28, 31.

35. Cullmann, *Christology*, pp. 29-30, 38-42.

century; a prophet claiming to be Moses *redivivus* attempted to re-enact the Exodus.[36]

Prophetic Christology in the Early Church

Prophetic activity was a widespread phenomenon in the early Church,[37] but prophetic Christology was not. The identification of Jesus as a prophet gave way to other titles of honor. Oscar Cullmann argued that the title was eventually abandoned because

> the concept of the eschatological Prophet is too narrow to do justice to the early Christian faith in Jesus Christ. It fully comprehends only one aspect of the earthly life of Jesus, and even in this aspect it can be supplemented by other more central concepts such as that of the Suffering Servant of God. Moreover, the concept of the Prophet cannot be united at all with those Christological titles of honour which refer to the present Lord, since it excludes by definition an interim following Easter. It is fundamentally incompatible with the perspective in which the whole New Testament sees the event of salvation.[38]

The major exception to this pattern of reticence and suppression was the Sayings Tradition designated as Q. Central to Jesus' identity in the Sayings Tradition is his activity as a prophet of God. A primary element in the world-view of Q is the idea that God has sent a long line of messengers to Israel. These agents have been rejected, abused, killed (Lk. 11.49-51/Mt. 23.34-36; Lk. 13.34/Mt. 23.37). John and Jesus belong to this line of witnesses (Lk. 7.31-35/Mt. 11.16-19). John appears as a dramatic prophet calling Israel to repentence, but Jesus is greater than John (Lk. 3.16/Mt. 3.11). John marks the culmination of the law and the prophets; Jesus marks the inauguration of the kingdom (Lk. 16.16/Mt. 11.12-13). Thus, John, and even more so Jesus, stands at the end of a long line of rejected messengers whom God sent to Israel. The activity of Jesus marks the final call of God to salvation. How one responds to Jesus and his messengers determines one's ultimate destiny. Jesus is the final prophet sent from God. He inaugurates the kingdom of God and issues the ultimate summons to salvation. Through this activity Jesus fulfills a long expectation in Israel. Without saying so directly, Q presents Jesus as the final, eschatological prophet whom

36. R. Meyer, 'προφήτης', *TDNT*, VI, pp. 796-828 (827).
37. See the discussion by Aune, *Prophecy*, pp. 189-231.
38. Cullmann, *Christology*, p. 49.

God has raised up in the line of Moses (Deut. 18.15). The message of Q is clear: 'you shall heed such a prophet' (Deut. 18.15).

One other major line of prophetic Christology survives in the material from early Christianity; this concept belongs uniquely to Jewish Christianity. In his commentary on Isaiah, Jerome cites the Jewish *Gospel of the Hebrews*:

> ...according to the Gospel written in the Hebrew speech, which the Nazarenes read, 'There shall descend upon him the whole fount of the Holy Spirit'... In the Gospel I mentioned above, I find this written: And it came to pass when the Lord was come up out of the water, the whole fount of the Holy Spirit descended and rested upon him, and said unto him: My son, in all the prophets was I waiting for thee that thou shouldst come, and I might rest in thee. For thou art my rest, thou art my first begotten son, that reignest for ever.[39]

Here Jesus is not only the prophet of God, but the recapitulation and consummation of all prophecy. This prophetic identity is uniquely linked to the presence of the Spirit upon Jesus.

This prophetic Christology is found in more detail in the *Kerygmata Petrou*.[40] G. Strecker characterizes the *Kerygmata Petrou* in this manner:

39. See M.R. James, *The Apocryphal New Testament* (Oxford: Clarendon Press, 1924), p. 5.

40. Prophetic Christology is given various expressions in the *Kerygmata Petrou*:

the prophet	*Hom.* 3.13.1; 10.4.3; 11.26.2; 11.35.3; 13.14.3
the true prophet	*Hom.* 3.13.2; 10.3.3; *Recg.* 3.41.4; 5.2.5, 9, 10; 6.14
the prophet of truth	*Hom.* 7.6.2; 11.19.1; 12.29.1; *Recg.* 1.44.5-6; cf. *Hom* 8.24.4.
the only true prophet	*Hom.* 7.8.1
the prophet at the right hand (of God)	*Hom* 7.11.3
the unerring prophet	*Hom.* 11.33.1; cf. 3.30.2
the good prophet	*Recg.* 1.40.1
the one prophet	*Recg.* 1.50.7; 54.5
unus verus propheta	*Recg.* 1.54; 4.35
verus propheta	*Recg.* 4.36
justus et verus propheta	*Recg.* 9.29

Most significantly, Jesus is identified as the fulfillment of Deut. 18.15 in *Hom.* 3.53.3.

The dominating entity in the Kerygmata is 'the true prophet,' the bearer of divine revelation, who has manifested himself since the beginning of the world in a continuous series of changing characters. Adam represents the first incarnation of 'the prophet'; he was anointed with the oil of the tree of life and possessed the Spirit of God; accordingly, contrary to the report in Genesis, he committed no sin. Beside him as figures in whom the true prophet was manifested prominence is given to the lawgiver Moses and the Lord Jesus. The true prophet has the task of proclaiming the 'lawful knowledge' which shows the way to the future aeon.[41]

Various aspects of gnostic thought are employed in this presentation. Feminine prophecy is considered false prophecy. The true prophet has always been preceded and shadowed by a false prophet; this pattern sets John the Baptist in opposition to Jesus, the true prophet.[42] The polemic addressed against the disciples of the Baptist in the Gospel of John—John disclaims the prophet title because Jesus is the true prophet (Jn 1.20-21, 25)—has now become a strong polemic against the Baptist himself.[43]

Oscar Cullmann seeks to formulate the prophetic Christology of this group. He says:

We see that this whole Jewish Christian teaching orients its positive as well as its polemic element around the concept of the Prophet. Despite the fact that the eschatological character which clings to this concept in Judaism and also in the New Testament recedes to a great extent, nevertheless we discover here the only explicitly developed Christology which rests on the old conception of the returning Prophet. It is without doubt one of the oldest Christologies we possess.[44]

This prophetic Christology was to have little further influence in the development of Christian theology. Its impact on the formation of Islam has been argued by some.[45]

Summation

The presentation of Jesus as a prophet in the Gospel of Mark operates against the backdrop of a broad and complex historical line of devel-

41. G. Strecker, 'The Kerygmata Petrou', in W. Schneemelcher (ed.), *New Testament Apocrypha* (2 vols.; Philadelphia: Westminster Press, 1965 [1964]), II, pp. 102-11 (107).
42. Strecker, 'The Kerygmata Petrou', pp. 106-11.
43. Cullmann, *Christology*, pp. 41-42.
44. Cullmann, *Christology*, p. 42.
45. Cullmann, *Christology*, pp. 42, 49-50.

opment. Prophecy as divination played a common role in daily events
of Greco-Roman life. Within the Greco-Roman mystery cults ecstatic
oracles played a central role. While this type of prophetic activity
exerted minimal influence upon Jewish and Christian prophecy, Greco-
Roman activity demonstrates the larger world-view into which Jewish
and Christian prophecy emerges.

The prophecy of ancient Israel exerts more influence upon prophetic
Christology. Israelite prophecy was complex and polymorphic. While
some forms of divination endured, more typical forms of prophecy
were found in shamanistic prophets, cult and Temple prophets, court
prophets, free-standing prophets and in prophetic literature.

Early Judaism provides closer antecedants to prophetic Christology.
Two types of non-eschatological prophecy are found in this period: the
clerical prophecy associated with priestly groups and the sapiential
prophecy practiced by rabbinic groups and by Philo. Eschatological
prophecy took both apocalyptic and non-apocalyptic forms. Apocalyptic prophecy emerges from classical prophecy and is marked by its
focus on visionary experiences which precede a final disruption and
renewal of the cosmos. The non-apocalyptic expectation for an eschatological prophet draws upon Deut. 18.15 and Mal. 3.1; 4.5-6. Typically the reappearance of a Moses or Elijah figure will mark the coming
of Yahweh. Three major figures embody this expectation in early
Judaism: the Teacher of Righteousness from Qumran, John the Baptist,
and, in some circles, Jesus of Nazareth.

Most scholars have argued that prophetic Christology played a limited and short-lived role in the New Testament period. Whatever
prophetic Christology underlies the synoptic tradition seems to have
been largely suppressed, replaced or incorporated. The Sayings Tradition likely carried a strong focus on Jesus as prophet, and a limited
form of prophetic Christology seems to survive in Lukan and Johannine
thought.

Prophetic Christology endured only in limited arenas. The prophetic
Christology associated with John the Baptist seems to survive among
disciples of the Baptist and later to merge into Mandean sects. The
Gospel of the Hebrews and the *Kerygmata Petrou* view Jesus as the
prophet in whom all prophecy is taken up and consummated. Jewish
Christianity ceased as a movement, and prophetic Christology played
no central role in the ongoing development of Christian thought.

The Literary Foreground

The title of Prophet (προφήτης) is not an explicit title for Jesus in the Gospel of Mark. Nonetheless the narrative constructs a clear characterization of Jesus as God's authentic Prophet.

Distribution

The Prophet title is related to Jesus on four occasions. In Mk 6.4 Jesus sets a proverb before the worshipers in his home town: 'A prophet is not without honor except in his home town and among his own people and in his own house.' This saying directly interprets the events in the synagogue when the people are scandalized by the presence and the message of Jesus (6.1-3).

Other passages feed the speculation that Jesus is a prophet. The growing report of Jesus' activity raises the issue of his identity. Herod and others see here the raising of the executed prophet, John the Baptist (6.14, 16). Alternate opinions find in Jesus the raised Elijah or a prophet like those of the Old Testament (6.15). Significantly, all forms of this speculation—the Baptist, Elijah, another prophet—center around a prophetic identity.

This same conjecture arises in the scene at Caesarea Philippi (8.27-30). When asked about popular views of Jesus' identity, the disciples list various opinions, all of which are prophetic: that he is John the Baptist, Elijah, one of the prophets.

Two key lines of prophetic expectation merge in the images of Mk 9.2-8, though the title itself is missing. In the presence of Moses and Elijah, Jesus is declared from heaven as the Beloved Son whom disciples are to obey. This scene suggests the whole spectrum of Old Testament prophecy reaches its fulfillment in Jesus. This prophetic imagery is accompanied by a sharp focus on suffering and death (9.9-13).

This popular speculation emerges finally in the abuse following the trial before the religious authorities (14.65). Here Jesus is mocked with a single taunt: 'Prophesy!' Thus, the image of the rejected prophet put forward at the beginning of Jesus' ministry is fulfilled in the passion story.

Association

Key concepts are associated with this prophetic image. In Mk 6.1-6 the people are scandalized by Jesus' activity in the synagogue. This rejection of Jesus is accompanied by a lack of wonders (6.5), by amazement at the unbelief of the people (6.6), and by Jesus' departure to teach in other villages (6.6). An important association lies close at hand in this proverb: Jesus identifies his mission as that of a rejected prophet of Israel.

The speculation in Mk 6.14-16 and 8.27-30 is associated with a growing interest in the identity of Jesus, both among the crowds and among the rulers. Suggested answers to this speculation arise from prophetic categories.

With the taunt of the soldiers for a word of prophecy, the association with the rejected prophet is renewed and acted out in the first trial of Jesus (14.53-65). The prophetic image developed in earlier stories comes to full expression in this scene. Standing before the religious leadership of Israel, Jesus is clearly portrayed as one who claims to speak for God. The trial focuses on the truth of this assertion. Various elements confirm the prophetic claim. Witnesses say he spoke of the fall of the Temple (Mk 14.58). Jesus tells of the future coming of the Son of Man (14.62). The words of Jesus provide fulfillment of the Old Testament (Dan. 7.13; Ps. 110.1). Lest the reader miss the imagery, those who torture Jesus mock him as one who claims the gift of prophecy (14.65). Thus, the presence of the prophetic claim is explicit. At the same time the story makes clear the rejection of this claim by the religious authorities. As a consequence the image of Jesus as a prophet stands near to the trial scene. Jesus, through his own words and deeds, has claimed to speak for Yahweh. This claim is rejected by the religious leaders of Israel, and Jesus is condemned to death as one who blasphemes the name of God.

Thus, two lines of association emerge around the prophetic imagery. In one stream Jesus is the object of popular speculation, and prophetic categories provide the first guesses at his identity. In the other stream Jesus sets forth his identity as a rejected prophet, then realizes that identity in the drama of his trial.

Confirmation

The narrative connects the proverb of Mk 6.4 directly to Jesus and his destiny. As the story demonstrates, it is Jesus who is rejected by his own, then moves on to others (6.1-3, 5-6). This proverb is emphasized when it is narrated from the lips of Jesus himself. In this way the narrative confirms the image of Jesus as the rejected prophet of God.

The speculation in Mk 6.14-16 and 8.27-30 is not directly confirmed, nor is it denied. Nonetheless this speculation has been prefaced by the story of Mk 6.1-6. The people thus wonder about something already confirmed for the reader of this Gospel.

In a similar way the drama of Jesus' first trial (Mk 14.53-65) completes the image of the rejected prophet set forth in 6.1-6. Here the confirmation is an ironic one: the taunt of the soldiers realizes the imagery set forth in Jesus' home town. Thus, the confirmation of Jesus as the rejected prophet in Mk 6.1-6 provides the backdrop against which to read later images.

Development
Despite the infrequent and indirect use of this title, the image of Jesus as the Prophet plays a decisive role in the larger narrative and its portrait of Jesus. The itinerant ministry of Jesus is narrated against the backdrop of the rejection in his home town (Mk 6.1-6). In response to this rejection Jesus goes to other villages and teaches (6.6b), then sends his disciples to replicate his ministry (6.7-13). These strategic connections insist that the itinerant ministry of Jesus in Galilee is that of a prophet whom Israel rejects at its own risk. This pattern set out near the beginning of Jesus' ministry and cast over the whole of his Galilean journey is confirmed at the end of his ministry. In the parable of the vineyard (12.1-12), the Son stands as the consummation of a long line of rejected messengers whom God has sent to Israel.

The prophetic imagery cast over the ministry of Jesus comes into sharper perspective in the story of Jesus' death. Mark 14–16 employs the death story to give surprising focus to the role of Jesus as the true Prophet of God. Through this process the passion story highlights an image of Jesus missing from other traditions of his death.[46] The prophetic Christology in Mark 14–16 is developed around three distinct roles: instruction, prediction and suffering.

The prophetic activity of Jesus provides instruction for his disciples. His words guide, correct and encourage his followers through the scenes of his passion. He serves for his disciples as Teacher (14.14, 49)

---

46. See the traditions of Jesus' death in Acts 2.14-36; 4.8-12; 10.34-43; 13.16-41; 17.22-31; 26.22-23; 1 Thess. 4.13-18; Rom. 1.1-6; Gal. 6.14; Phil. 2.5-11; 1 Cor. 15.3-7; 2 Tim. 1.8-10; Tit. 2.11-14; Eph. 1.3-14; Col. 1.13-23; Heb. 10.1-25; 1 Pet. 1.3-5; 1 Jn 1.5-10; 5.6; Rev. 1.4-7; 5.1-14; the prophetic image is mentioned but not developed in Lk. 24.19-27; Acts 3.22; 7.37.

and Rabbi (14.45). Through his words Jesus interprets his own identity: he is the Messiah (14.6-8, 61-62); the bringer of a new covenant (14.24); the Son of Man (14.21, 41, 62); the Son of God (14.36, 61); the shepherd of God's flock (14.27); the fulfillment of the Old Testament (14.49). Jesus further instructs the disciples about his destiny: he will die and be buried (14.8); he will be betrayed (14.18-21, 41); his blood will be shed and his body broken (14.22-25); he will be abandoned by his own (14.27, 30); he will be raised and go to Galilee (14.28). Jesus also interprets for his disciples various events and symbols which surround his passion: the woman has anointed him for burial (14.8); the bread and cup of Passover portray the death of Jesus (14.22-25); the relation of Jesus' arrest and death to the Scriptures is shown (14.49; 15.34). Through these elements the passion scenes provide an implicit image of Jesus as the teaching Prophet who guides his followers through his final days.

An extended line of predictions about the future confirms the image of Jesus as the Prophet of God. Various sayings have immediate fulfillment: the Passover preparation (14.13-16); the coming of the betrayer (14.41-42). Thus, the narrative places a paradigm of prediction/fulfillment at the beginning of the passion and surrounds the words of Jesus with an aura of certainty. Other predictions are fulfilled in the subsequent events of the narrative: the disciples fall away (14.27, 50); Peter denies Jesus (14.30, 66-72); Jesus is betrayed by one of the Twelve (14.18, 43-46); the Scriptures are fulfilled (14.21, 27, 49; 15.34); Jesus is struck down, killed, buried. These transactions extend the prediction/fulfillment schema and confirm the identity of Jesus as the authentic Prophet of God. Various other predictions remain unfulfilled within the narrative, but the reader is encouraged to see these as authentic prophecy: Jesus will go before them into Galilee (14.28; 16.7); the gospel will be preached throughout the world (14.9); the Son of Man will come with the clouds of heaven (14.62); Jesus will celebrate anew in the kingdom (14.25). Thus, Jesus' predictions characterize him as the true prophetic voice sent from God.

The passion narrative also characterizes Jesus as a suffering prophet and the suffering Just One. The theme of Jesus' instruction is his destiny of suffering and death (14.8, 18-21, 22-25, 27, 28, 30, 41, 49). Jesus' predictions center on his passion (14.18, 27, 30). In addition, various texts draw upon the prophetic image of the Suffering Servant (14.53-65; 15.1-15, 16-20b, 20c-37). This image of Jesus as the suffering, righteous, rejected Prophet is made explicit in the scene of abuse: 'And some began to spit upon him and to cover his face and to strike him and to say to him, "Prophesy!" And the guards received him with blows' (Mk 14.65).

These three lines converge in the saying of Mk 10.45. This logion concludes the focused instruction on service and discipleship (10.42-45) and informs followers of the role of the Son of Man. This saying also foretells the destiny of the Son of Man. At the center of this prophecy is his death for the people.

Effect

The effect of this literary strategy is decisive. Building upon the rejection in his home town, Jesus' itinerant ministry and his scandalous death are sketched as the story of God's rejected Prophet. A literary enigma results: apart from any direct confessional use of the title a clear prophetic image of Jesus is developed within the world of this narrative. This irony likely reflects the historical reality behind the early Christian tradition. As Cullmann notes, the early Church was reticent to confess or even to admit the identity of Jesus as a prophet because of its post-Easter Christology.[47] Cullmann concludes of this prophetic characterization: 'It is without doubt one of the oldest Christologies we possess.'[48] Indeed, if the self-understanding of Jesus is thoroughly immersed in Judaism and the Old Testament, then prophetic Christology would provide the simplest and nearest pattern for his understanding of his work and identity. A stark irony seems to emerge from behind prophetic Christology: the title used by earliest Christians and perhaps by Jesus himself was absorbed and suppressed within later Christian confessions.

The formal literary strategy at work in the Gospel of Mark reflects both aspects of this irony. While the story makes no confession of Jesus as Prophet and never explicitly affirms the title, a strong prophetic Christology emerges through the structure and strategy of the narrative.

Conclusion

Drawing upon a clear line of Jewish expectation, the Gospel of Mark sketches a vivid portrait of Jesus as the rejected Prophet of the end

---

47. Cullmann, *Christology*, p. 49.
48. Cullmann, *Christology*, p. 42.

time. This image emerges from complex transactions within the narrative rather than from an explicit use of the Prophet title. Through the
synagogue drama of Mk 6.1-6 Jesus is characterized as a rejected
prophet of God. This imagery is cast over the Galilean ministry and
consummated in the parable of the vineyard (12.1-12). This prophetic
imagery comes into sharp focus in the story of Jesus' death. Despite the
absence of the title in Mark 14–16, the passion narrative employs
instruction, prediction and suffering to show Jesus as the true messenger of God. This portrait wraps Jesus in the garments of the Old Testament prophets[49] and presents him as the last of God's messengers
(12.1-12). In this way a title quickly abandoned by the early Church
nonetheless plays a central role in the characterization of Jesus in the
Gospel of Mark.

49. See, for example, the combination of instruction, prediction and suffering
present in Moses, Elijah, Hosea and Jeremiah. For a thorough treatment of the suffering of the prophets, see Odil Hannes Steck, *Israel und das gewaltsame Geschick
der Propheten: Untersuchungen zur Überlieferung des deuteronomistischen Ges-
chichstbildes im Alten Testament, Spätjudentum und Urchristentum* (WMANT, 23;
Neukirchen–Vluyn: Neukirchener Verlag, 1967).

Chapter 4

THE GREATER ONE

> And he was preaching saying, 'After me comes the one greater than
> me...' (Mk 1.7).

The designation of Jesus as the Greater One (ὁ ἰσχυρότερός) is a literary legacy of the Baptist tradition. The description is used once in the
preaching of John to clarify the status and function of Jesus (Mk 1.7).
Indeed, this is the only term employed by John to describe Jesus in the
Gospel of Mark. Its sole association within this Gospel is with the
status of John. The validity of the title is confirmed through its speaker
and its context: it belongs to the preaching of the Baptist. The only
pattern of development is found in the explication of this claim in
Mk 1.8.

The effect of this title upon the narrative far outweighs it profile. It is
clear that the background of this term does not lie in the Old Testament
or in the thought world of Judaism: it belongs rather to the history of
early Christianity. Throughout its development Christianity struggled to
define the identity of John and to clarify his relation to Jesus.[1] The
Gospel of Mark unfolds this relationship in a few lines and a single
title. John came before Jesus, but Jesus is greater than John. The
relationship is that of servant to master, and the ministry of Jesus exceeds that of the Baptist (1.7-8). This superiority is symbolized through
the contrasting modes of baptism which they offer: John baptizes in
water, but Jesus will baptize in the Spirit. The narrative insists that this
evaluation is not imposed from beyond, but emerges in the preaching of
John. Thus, the value of this term is wholly relational: it sets the pattern
for the connection between Jesus and John the Baptist.

---

1. This debate can be seen behind various Gospel traditions and in texts such
as the Pseudo-Clementines. See the discussion in Chapter 3 on traditions concerning John the Baptist.

A secondary effect is produced by this connection. Since John is characterized as the prophet *par excellence*, it is precisely in his prophetic activity that Jesus surpasses the Baptist. Jesus comes after John; thus he stands at the end of the prophetic tradition. Conversely, Jesus surpasses the work of John; thus he culminates the prophetic tradition. This characterization confirms the larger portrait of Jesus as God's true Prophet.[2] This portrait is acted out in the parable of the vineyard (Mk 12.1-12): many messengers are sent and rejected, one is wounded in the head (Mk 12.4; see 6.7). At the end of this line comes the Beloved Son (12.6; see 1.11).

As a result of these narrative patterns the naming of Jesus as the Greater One serves an important role in the strategy of this Gospel. Confirmed by the Baptist as a term which clarifies his relation to Jesus, the Greater One title is ultimately a tool of characterization. Jesus, who follows in the wake of John, is the Prophet whose status and ministry surpasses that of the Baptist. He is the last and greatest of God's messengers.

2.   See Chapter 3 on the characterization of Jesus as God's Prophet.

Chapter 5

PRIEST

And Jesus, seeing his faith, says to the paralytic, 'Child, your sins are forgiven' (Mk 2.5).

The office of priest played a decisive role in the religious structures of the Greco-Roman world and in Judaism. Within areas of Judaism there developed divergent expectations of a priestly messiah. Priestly images emerge in a distinct way in the characterization of Jesus in the Gospel of Mark.

The Historical Background

Within Judaism arose a line of expectation for an eschatological, messianic high priest in the image of Melchizedek. The cessation of the levitical line of priests with the Exile encouraged the transfer of hope to the mysterious Melchizedek figure and to an eschatological priesthood not bound by the limits of political and historical reality.

This hope drew upon two obscure references. In Gen. 14.7 Melchizedek represents a mysterious king before whom Abraham paid homage. As with other Canaanite leaders, Melchizedek was supposed to be both priest and king. Psalm 110 anoints the leader of Israel with the mantle of Melchizedek. The priesthood of the Jewish king is to be eternal (110.4), and it expects the vindication of Yahweh (110.1, 5-7). Oscar Cullmann sees here the origin of priestly Christology:

> In so far as the idea of kingship is the basis of messianism and in so far as Ps. 110 connects this kingship with an ideal priesthood, we have here the starting-point for a messianic formulation of the figure of the High Priest.[1]

The use of this concept may be seen at various points in Jewish and Christian thought.

1. Cullmann, *Christology*, p. 84.

Psalm 110

That Psalm 110 is understood as a messianic hymn is evident from Mk 12.35-37 and from its extensive use in the New Testament (Mt. 22.24; 26.64; Mk 12.36; 14.62; 16.19; Lk. 20.42; 22.69; Acts 2.34; Rom. 2.5; 8.34; 11.29; 1 Cor. 15.25; Eph. 1.20; Col. 3.1; Heb. 1.3, 13; 5.6, 10; 6.20; 7.3, 11, 15, 17, 21; 8.1; 10.12). Within this messianic exegesis a limited number of passages focus the Melchizedek connection (Heb. 5.6,10; 6.20; 7.3, 11, 15, 17, 21).

The Epistle to the Hebrews

The Epistle to the Hebrews develops a priestly Christology which unites the work of Jesus to the Melchizedek imagery. This exegesis is framed by two direct citations of Ps. 110.4 from the Septuagint (Heb. 5.6; 7.21). This framework establishes the priesthood of Jesus after the order of Melchizedek. Within this framework various aspects of Jesus' priesthood are developed. In Heb. 5.10 and 6.20 Jesus has become not only Priest, but High Priest—a reference missing from Psalm 110. Hebrews 7.3 wraps this function in timeless mystery—it is without beginning or end. In Heb. 7.11, 15-17 the superiority of this priesthood over all others is focused. Thus, Hebrews employs Ps. 110.4 and the shadowy image of Melchizedek to construct a crucial strata of its Christology: Jesus has been established by God as the eternal and unsurpassable High Priest.

Qumran

Some documents from Qumran expect a priestly messiah. Distinguished from the political and royal messiah of Judah and Israel is the priestly messiah. Known as the messiah of Aaron or the messiah of Levi, this figure will take priority over the political messiah, and he will guide the purity of the eschatological community (1QSa 2.18-21). Scriptural support for this dual messiahship is found in Zechariah 4 and in Num. 24.17.[2] In addition, the Teacher of Righteousness has both priestly and eschatological dimensions (1QpHab 2.8).

---

2. See E. Lohse, *The New Testament Environment* (London: SCM Press, 1976 [1974]), p. 108. See also K.G. Kuhn, 'The Two Messiahs of Aaron and Israel', in K. Stendahl (ed.), *The Scrolls and the New Testament* (London: SCM Press, 1958), pp. 54-64.

Other Traditions

The image of a messianic priest emerges at scattered points of Jewish tradition. In a midrash to the Song of Solomon (*Midr. Cant.* 100b), the eschatological priest-king serves a mediating role.[3] Elijah appears as end time priest in some literature.[4] Some Adam speculation idealizes the role of the priest-king.[5] The return of Elijah is sometimes accompanied by an eschatological priest.[6] Philo links the Logos to the Melchizedek figure and refers to him as the priest of God.[7] Ernst Käsemann argues for a Melchizedek speculation which exists prior to the book of Hebrews and is of mixed origin.[8] The Melchizedek speculation emerges among various church fathers.[9]

Thus the Melchizedek imagery of Genesis 14 and Psalm 110 sponsors within Judaism vague speculation concerning a priestly messianic figure. This idealized eschatological priesthood provides a clear antithesis and replacement of the historical priesthood of Israel. Within the New Testament, only the Epistle to the Hebrews poses a priestly Christology around the Melchizedek speculation.

The Literary Foreground

The priest title (ἱερεύς) is never applied to Jesus in the Gospel of Mark, and the Melchizedek speculation is never employed. Despite this absence the narrative strategy at work in the Gospel of Mark generates an unusual priestly image around the character of Jesus. This priestly image, though briefly developed, has been woven into the larger tapestry of the Gospel of Mark and contributes to its wider christological portrait.

3.   See Cullmann, *Christology*, p. 85.

4.   See J. Jeremias, ''Ηλ(ε)ίας', *TDNT*, II, pp. 934-41; See also Str–B, IV, pp. 460-65.

5.   See F.J. Jerome, 'Das geschichtliche Melchisedek-Bild und seine Bedeutung im Hebräerbrief' (unpublished doctoral dissertation, Freiburg University, 1927).

6.   See Str–B, IV, pp. 460-65.

7.   *Leg. All.* 3.79; *Congr.* 99.

8.   E. Käsemann, *Das wandernde Gottesvolk: Eine Untersuchung. zum Hebräerbrief* (Göttingen: Vandenhoeck & Ruprecht, 1939), p. 130.

9.   See G. Bardy, 'Melchisedek dans la tradition patristique', *RB* 35 (1926), pp. 496-509; 36 (1927), pp. 25-45.

This priestly image of Jesus is developed through four closely related passages: Mk 1.39-45; 2.1-13; 2.23-28; 3.1-7a. The concentration of these stories within the same unit (Mk 1.1–3.7a) provides a decisive narrative impact. (1) The fourfold repetition within the initial unit establishes the priestly role of Jesus as a significant element for both plot and characterization.[10] (2) The close proximity of the stories not only reinforces the theme, but also creates a process of development.[11] Each story contributes a different shading to the priestly imagery. (3) Beyond this, the four stories develop the priestly Christology over against a central plot element—the opposition to Jesus by the religious leaders. Through this connection the failure of the religious leaders is crystallized by the developing images of Jesus as authentic Priest for God's people. In addition to these stories in 3.1-7a, the priestly portrait is also found in Mk 7.14-23.

Mark 1.39-45: Healing a Leper
Following the paradigmatic day in Capernaum which opens his service (Mk 1.21-39), Jesus begins an itinerant ministry throughout Galilee. In the initial account of his journey (Mk 1.39-45), Jesus is confronted by a leper. The healing of the leper is accomplished by two elements: the healing touch (ἥψατο) and the healing pronouncement (καταρίσθητι).

Significantly, the Old Testament code reserves both the healing ritual and the healing pronouncement for priests (Lev. 13–14). The instructions to Moses are clear:

> This shall be the law of the leper for the day of his cleansing. He shall be brought to the priest; and the priest shall go out of the camp, and the priest shall make an examination. Then, if the leprous disease is healed

10. Two literary traits establish this priority. (1) The Gospel of Mark tends to focus primary themes in opening units. Mk 1.1-20, for example, establishes the major themes of the Gospel. These initial images cast a long and distinct shadow across the larger narrative. In a similar manner, the concentrated focus of Jesus' priestly deeds in Mk 1.1–3.7a creates a strong primacy effect. (2) The Gospel of Mark repeats crucial events, typically in triads. The fourfold repetition of priestly images in 1.1–3.7a belongs to this pattern of reinforcement and intensification. Thus, the priestly image is established early and etched deeply into the story of Jesus.

11. Typically, the Gospel of Mark employs a triadic structure of repetition to provide intensification. See, for example, the prayers of Jesus in Gethsemane (14.32-42) and the denial by Peter (14.66-72). On the role of narrative triads, see Rhoads and Michie, *Mark as Story*, pp. 54-55.

in the leper, the priest shall command them to take for him who is to be cleansed two living clean birds and cedarwood and scarlet stuff and hyssop; and the priest shall command them to kill one of the birds in an earthen vessel over running water. He shall take the living bird with the cedarwood and the scarlet stuff and the hyssop, and dip them and the living bird in the blood of the bird that was killed over the running water; and he shall sprinkle it seven times upon him who is to be cleansed of leprosy; then he shall pronounce him clean, and shall let the living bird go into the open field (Lev. 14.1-20).

The Mishnah describes the same healing rite (*Neg.* 14.1-3), and it confirms the unique role of the priest: 'All are qualified to inspect leprosy-signs, but only a priest may pronounce them clean or unclean' (*Neg.* 3.1).

In contrast to this line of cultic tradition, Mk 1.41-42 assigns both the healing and the pronouncement to Jesus: '...he touched and he says to him, "I am willing. Be made clean." And immediately the leprosy departed from him, and he was made clean.' The imagery is clear: Jesus functions in this story—apart from the Temple and its lineage—as the priestly servant of God.[12]

Jesus' priestly deed represents a radical break with tradition, and it provides a stark contrast to the behavior of priests of Israel. Following the cleansing, the leper is sent as a witness. Jesus sends the one declared clean specifically to the religious authority which had declared the leper unclean. There the leper is to bear witness to the power of Jesus and, by implication, to the impotence of the priest. This witness is not to be read as to the authorities,[13] but as a clear witness against them.[14] This use of αὐτοῖς is wholly within the operative range of the dative case,[15] and similar use is suggested by various synoptic passages (Mk 6.11; 10.34; 13.9; Lk. 4.22). The clearest parallel is found in Mt. 23.31, where the religious authorities condemn themselves: 'So that you are bearing witness against yourselves [ὥστε μαρτυρεῖτε ἑαυτοῖς] that you are the sons of the ones killing the prophets.'

---

12. Healing outside the Temple cult also belongs to the prophetic tradition. See, for example, Exod. 4.6-7; 2 Kgs 4.32-37.

13. The RSV ranges far afield with its translation of εἰς μαρτύριον αὐτοῖς as 'for a proof to the people'.

14. I have argued in detail for a negative reading of this witness in 'Mark 1,44: The Witness of the Leper', *ZNW* 83 (1992), pp. 257-65.

15. See, for example, A.T. Robertson, *A Grammar of the Greek New Testament in the Light of Historical Research* (Nashville: Broadman, 1934), pp. 538-39.

This negative reading of the witness may help to clarify the empassioned commands of Jesus: he is moved to anger by the religious hypocrisy which declares this person unclean but cannot heal the leper.[16] This witness of condemnation also sparks the controversy between Jesus and the religious authorities. Beyond this, the witness of the leper to the power of Jesus cannot be silenced. Instead, the leper proclaims widely and draws people from everywhere to Jesus (1.45).

Thus, Mk 1.39-45 generates a number of important images. (1) Jesus is shown to have power to heal and cleanse a leper—a feat more difficult than raising the dead in the evaluation of the rabbis.[17] (2) Beyond this, the healing action of Jesus creates a sharp controversy with the religious authorities—a controversy that is heightened in Mk 1.1-3.7a and played out in the larger context of the passion. The leper is sent to those who have declared him or her unclean but are powerless to heal. At the altar of Israel, the leper is to demonstrate the power of Jesus both to heal and to pronounce clean. (3) The christological imagery produced by this account proves significant. Jesus does what only a priest of God can do, but, ironically, what the priests of Israel have not done. The priestly images generated by the account center the controversy not simply in an isolated deed of Jesus, but in his very identity—he is the priestly servant of God whose deeds are marked by power and compassion. Because the controversy is linked to the larger identity of Jesus, this conflict will be an ongoing theme.

Mark 2.1-13: Offering God's Forgiveness

The priestly role of Jesus emerges from a second healing account in Mk 2.1-13. While the story initially focuses on the healing of a paralytic, an extended plot digression (2.6-11) makes the controversy with the scribes the focus of the story. Thus, the story is best labeled as a healing/controversy.

The expected plot line is interrupted at the very point of the healing. While the disease provides the initial opposition to Jesus, a new opponent—the scribes—is presented in the midst of the account. The scribes now occupy a place of opposition usually reserved for disease or demons. This subtle transition alerts the reader to the deep chasm which is drawn between Jesus and the religious authorities in the

16. The more difficult reading of anger (ὀργισθείς) is to be preferred to mercy (σπλαγανισθείς).

17. See Str–B, IV.2, p. 745.

Gospel of Mark. The conflict is played out in the actions of the scribes: they grumble against Jesus and accuse him of blasphemy (2.6-7). As a consequence Mk 2.1-13 presents two crucial themes: the power of Jesus to heal and the controversy which results.

Against the backdrop of Jesus' healing and controversy with the religious authorities, Mk 2.1-13 adds a priestly image to the portrait of Jesus. The healing command is distinct: 'Child, your sins are forgiven.' This offer of forgiveness need not signal the presence of a second source or story.[18] Indeed, the linkage of sin and sickness is common to the world-view of the story. The controversy lies not in the offer of forgiveness in response to disease, but rather in who it is that declares the forgiveness. Jesus offers God's forgiveness of sins,[19] and this stirs the response of the religious authorities. The offer of forgiveness introduces a christological/theological debate which neither the story, nor apparently the early Church, resolves: does God alone forgive sins? Nonetheless, an important christological image emerges from the account: Jesus is the one empowered to offer God's forgiveness of sins.

In the worship of Israel the offer of God's forgiveness belongs to the priesthood.[20] The singular role of the priest in this process is clear:

> And the priest who is anointed and consecrated as priest in his father's place shall make atonement, wearing the holy linen garments; he shall make atonement for the sanctuary, and he shall make atonement for the tent of meeting and for the altar, and he shall make atonement for the priests and for the people of the assembly. And this shall be an everlasting statute for you, that atonement may be made for the people of Israel once in the year because of all their sins (Lev. 16.32-34).

Thus, Jesus does in Mk 2.1-13 what only a priest of God can do— offer God's forgiveness for sins.

---

18. Rudolf Bultmann, *History of the Synoptic Tradition* (trans. John Marsh; New York: Harper & Row, rev. edn, 1963), argued that 2.5b-10a is a secondary insertion of an apothegm into the traditional miracle story. Most scholars have accepted this division of the story.

19. The use of ἀφίενται is crucial. This form is best seen as a divine passive: 'Your sins are forgiven (by God)'. For use of the divine passive, see Rudolf Pesch, *Das Markusevangelium* (HTKNT; 2 vols.; Freiburg: Herder, 3rd edn, 1980), I, pp. 155-56; and BDF, p. 72.

20. See the atonement liturgy in Lev. 16. In addition, see the repeated formula of forgiveness in Lev. 4.26, 31, 35; 5.6, 10, 13, 18; 6.7. Prophets may also offer forgiveness (2 Sam. 12.13; Isa. 38.5, 17).

This radical claim to priestly power provides a sharp contrast to the authorities: Jesus does for the paralytic what the religious authorities have failed to do. Once again, this conflict is linked not only to the deeds of Jesus, but ultimately to his identity.

Mark 2.23-3.7a: Ministering on the Sabbath

Jesus' attitude concerning the sabbath is presented in two related incidents in Mk 2.23-38 and 3.1-7a. In Mk 2.23-28, Jesus defends his disciples' plucking of grain on the sabbath. Following the example of David, Jesus gives the need of his friends priority over the ritual observance of the sabbath: 'Have you never read what David did?... The sabbath exists for the sake of the person and not the person for the sabbath' (2.25, 27). Jesus thus permits his followers to do work on the sabbath—a privilege reserved by law for the priests of Israel. Significantly, this imagery is set over against the questioning of the Pharisees (2.24).

Mark 3.1-7a gives more decisive focus to this priestly function. Here Jesus takes the sabbath as an occasion for ministry to the people. In doing so Jesus appropriates for himself the levitical exemption from sabbath work laws. Jesus does what any good priest should do—he ministers to the people on the sabbath. In contrast, the leaders of Israel employ the sabbath to plot the death of Jesus (3.6). Mark 3.1-7a thus employs the priestly image to contrast Jesus and the religious leaders and to bring the controversy between them to a sharp climax. At the same time the story adds another priestly element to the christological portrait: Jesus works on the sabbath for the healing of the people.

Mark 7.14-23: Interpreting Food Laws

The teaching material of Mk 7.14-23 also links Jesus to a priestly role. Here Jesus reconstructs the traditional laws concerning clean/unclean. Clean/unclean was previously decided on the nature of the food which was eaten:

> Every animal that parts the hoof and has the hoof cloven in two, and chews the cud, among the animals, you may eat (Deut. 14.6).

> Of all that are in the waters you may eat these: whatever has fins and scales you may eat. And whatever does not have fins and scales you shall not eat; it is unclean for you (Deut. 14.9-10).

In a radical departure from these laws, Jesus establishes a new standard: it is not what enters a person that makes one clean/unclean, but what comes out of a person. Ethics, not eating, becomes the standard for clean/unclean. In Mk 7.14-23 it is Jesus who applies the standard of clean/unclean for the community of believers. In this manner the Gospel of Mark again employs a priestly image to characterize Jesus.

The Development and Effect of Priestly Christology
Despite the absence of the priestly title, the priestly role of Jesus has been identified in five passages (1.39-45; 2.1-13, 23-28; 3.1-7a; 7.14-23). These priestly christological images are limited in scope and should be considered a minor theme of the narrative. At the same time, these priestly images are not isolated from the larger plot and characterization of the Gospel of Mark. The narrative strategy weaves the priestly role of Jesus into the larger framework of this text in crucial ways. Two literary traits will demonstrate this pattern.

First, the priestly christological images are developed in correspondance with the religious controversy theme. The parameters of this conflict with religious authorities are established in Mk 1.1-3.7a. The first hint of this conflict emerges in 1.22, where the authority of Jesus' teaching contrasts that of the scribes. This contrast is focused in 1.44 by Jesus' command that the leper appear before the priest. The conflict becomes explicit in 2.6-7 when the scribes grumble at Jesus' offer of forgiveness. The controversy emerges anew in 2.16 over the issue of eating with sinners and in 2.18 over fasting. The debate over the sabbath emerges in 2.24. This opening line of conflict reaches its climax in the sabbath debate of 3.1-7a, which ends with a death plot (3.6) and the departure of Jesus (3.7a).

Thus, the religious controversy theme and the priestly Christology emerge from the same literary soil. A strong pattern of conflict is developed in 1.1–3.7a and serves as the backdrop for the Jerusalem conflict in chapters 11–16. Of the five instances of priestly Christology, four are narrated within the initial conflict paradigm of 1.1–3.7a. Conversely, the four priestly passages provide the backbone for this initial conflict model. Thus, religious controversy and priestly Christology are intricately linked in their development. Through this pattern a crucial literary standard may been isolated: the Gospel of Mark employs priestly christological images solely in correlation with and in response to the theme of Jesus' controversy with the religious leaders of Israel.

Secondly, because of this correlation with the controversy theme the priestly Christology is linked to the larger plot development of the narrative—particularly to the passion. Jesus' conflict with the religious authorities plays a crucial role in the plotting of this Gospel.[21] This conflict is prominent in the opening chapters (1.22, 44; 2.6-7, 16, 18, 24; 3.1-7a), but almost absent from Mark 4–10. Mark 11–13 provides the transition from Jesus' ministry to his passion by reintroducing this conflict to serve as the background for Jesus' suffering and death. Various literary devices are employed to narrate the conflict between Jesus and the Jerusalem Temple.[22]

This well-developed conflict theme has close links to the death of Jesus. The death plots and the arrest of Jesus are a narrative result of Jesus' opposition to the Temple.[23] Three trips to Jerusalem are marked by confrontation between Jesus and the Temple (11.11; 11.12-25; 11.27-33). The biting parable of the vineyard follows (12.1-12). These events, particularly the parable, lead to the death plot in Mk 12.12. In a similar manner, Jesus' Temple opposition provides the charge against him in Mk 14.58.

A strong literary connection emerges between Jesus' conflict with the religious authorities and his death. Because priestly images participate in the formative stages of this controversy (1.1–3.7a), the priestly Christology flows ultimately into the larger stream of passion Christology.

As a consequence the imagery of Jesus as Priest is limited, but not isolated. Each priestly element belongs to the setting of conflict with the leaders of Israel. This ongoing conflict plays a central role in the plot of the Gospel and leads ultimately to the passion narrative. Thus,

---

21. I have dealt with this issue more closely in 'Which Mountain Is "This Mountain"? A Critical Note on Mark 11.22-25', in *Paradigms* 2.1 (1986), pp. 33-38.

22. For example, (1) Jesus enters the Temple and looks about at everything, then departs. 'Looking about' has a sense of foreboding in this Gospel, and the departure of Jesus is equally symbolic. (2) The intercalation of the cursed fig tree and the Temple is provocative. (3) Various religious groups parade before Jesus to engage in conflict and debate. (4) A prophetic display is directed against the Temple in 11.15-17. (5) The parable of the vineyard and an Old Testament citation are directed against the religious leadership (12.1-12). (6) The destruction of the Temple is prophesied in Mk 13. (7) The replacement of the Temple as the center of worship is suggested in Mk 11.22-25.

23. For a detailed treatment, see John R. Donahue, *Are You the Christ? The Trial Narrative in the Gospel of Mark* (SBLDS, 10; Missoula, MT: University of Montana Press, 1973), pp. 103-38. See also the treatment by Kelber, 'From Passion Narrative to Gospel', pp. 168-72.

the limited portrayal of Jesus in a priestly function is a small but significant part of a larger narrative plot and of a larger narrative portrait of Jesus.

Conclusion

Despite the absence of the Priest title or any Melchizedek associations, the priestly role of Jesus provides a minor christological theme in the Gospel of Mark. This priestly imagery is always linked to the controversy with the religious leaders. Through this connection the priestly Christology participates in the larger plot line of this Gospel—particularly in the passion narrative. Beyond its significance as a christological image and its linkage to the larger plan of the Gospel, the priestly image likely served an important role in the life of the church which lived by this Gospel.

While it is improbable that Jesus understood or described himself in priestly terms, the priestly image of Jesus seems most relevant to a community witnessing the traumatic destruction of Jerusalem and its Temple. Two questions pressed upon this community. In light of their past they must answer the question 'Why are you no longer Jewish?' In response to their future they must answer the question 'How do we live in a world no longer Jewish?' The community which lives by the Gospel of Mark finds the answer to these troublesome questions in the stories of their faith, particularly in Jesus' conflict with the religious authorities. Because of this, the priestly role of Jesus proves vital for the ongoing life of the community.

Jesus' priestly deeds thus provided two crucial elements for the life of the believing community. First, the priestly role of Jesus helped believers to justify their identity over against a Jewish heritage and Jewish opponents. The events which culminated in 70 CE were seen as the final death throes of a city and a Temple that had long stood under the judgment of God. Jesus himself had denounced the Temple and its practices through his words and his deeds.[24] While the religious leaders, the Temple mountain, and the Temple cult embodied this failure, Jesus embodies the true faith of Israel for this community. The priestly role of Jesus thus provided a polemic by which the Church could justify

---

24. See Broadhead, 'Which Mountain?' for a full treatment of this condemnation.

their identity over against their own Jewish heritage and against Jewish opponents.

Secondly, the priestly role of Jesus helped to clarify the believers' mission in the wider Gentile world in which they found themselves. Jesus himself had replaced the Temple tradition with new patterns of worship, and this new life was continuing among his followers. Jesus' priestly service offered the paradigm for this new existence. This new worship was marked by mercy, power, healing and acceptance—as at the healing of the leper in Mk 1.39-45. This new worship was marked by the free offer of God's forgiveness—as at the healing of the paralytic in Mk 2.1-13. This new worship valued deeds of mercy over ritual—as in the stories of Jesus' ministry on the sabbath (Mk 2.23–3.7a). This new worship cared for ethics more than food laws—as in the debate in Mk 7.14-23. This new worship was marked by prayer and faith and forgiveness—see Mk 11.22-25. In the aftermath of the fall of the Temple the Christian community offered the world new patterns of worship. These patterns could be offered with authority because they had come from the ministry of Jesus. Thus, the priestly image of Jesus provided an apologetic for the ministry of the Church in the Gentile world in which they now lived.

This literary strategy sheds new light upon the role of the titles. While the Priest title is never employed and the Melchizedek imagery is not evoked, priestly imagery plays an important role in the characterization of Jesus in the Gospel of Mark. The image of Jesus as God's Priest to Israel is built around Jesus' deeds and constructed against the backdrop of the Old Testament. This minor christological theme has been linked by the narrative to the controversy with the religious leaders. This connection links the priestly characterization into the mainstream of the narrative plot and joins it to the passion narrative. While this strategy has a profound effect upon the literary characterization of Jesus, it may well reflect the historical and theological situation of the community which lived by the Gospel of Mark. Because it was rooted in the ministry of Jesus and woven into the framework of their Gospel, this priestly Christology proved decisive for the life of the believing community. The patterns observed around the image of the Priest are typical of the way in which the Gospel of Mark constructs both individual names for Jesus and its larger christological portrait.

Chapter 6

KING

And the inscription of his indictment was written above: 'The King of the Jews' (Mk 15.26).

The title of King has a common use among the nations of the ancient Near East. Within the Old Testament this concept is applied to Yahweh, then to an agent anointed by Yahweh to rule over Israel. Messianic hopes converge around the image of a future Davidic king, and the New Testament takes up this image in various forms.

The Historical Background

The concept of kingship in Israel is likely taken over from neighboring models. Oriental kings typically exercised both political and priestly roles, and they were understood to be physical children of the deity. Various aspects of this model emerge within the corporate life of Israel. Indeed, the Old Testament insists that human kingship is an office borrowed from Israel's neighbors (1 Sam. 8.4-5, 19-20).

Yahweh is the king of Israel (Isa. 6.5; Pss. 22.3-5; 24.7-10; 145.11). Three aspects of Yahweh's kingship are presented. Some passages speak of God's timeless reign over Israel (Exod. 15.18; 1 Sam. 12.12; Pss. 145.11; 146.10). Other passages look forward to a future reign which fulfills the ideals of Yahweh's kingship (Isa. 24.23; 33.22; Zeph. 3.15; Obad. 21; Zech. 14.16-19). A third category is built on cultic events and points to the present enthronement and reign of Yahweh over Israel and the nations (Pss. 47, 93, 96, 97, 99).

Yahweh's rule comes to be exercised through historical figures anointed to lead Israel. The establishment of the monarchy is a rejection of God's rule (1 Sam. 8.7), yet God assents to this (1 Sam. 8.22). Eventually the king is understood as one anointed and empowered by God to exercise political and spiritual leadership over Israel (Pss. 2, 21). This figure is designated as God's Son (Ps. 2.7).

The ideal model of Yahweh's anointed ruler is David. Both the quality (2 Sam. 8.13-15) and the extent (2 Sam. 7.12-16; Ps. 89) of his reign are seen in ideal terms. The Nathan prophecy of 2 Sam. 7.4-17 was understood to promise an unbroken line of Davidic kings. When historical circumstances intervened, the promise was seen in terms of the restoration of David's reign. In the absence of political power the hope of Israel was often focused on this future king. Different terms were used to connect this hope to David. The future king is known in Isa. 11.10 as the 'Sprout of Jesse' and in other places as the 'Shoot (of David)' (Jer. 23.5; 33.15; Zech. 3.8; 6.12). He is also known as 'David' in a figurative sense, since the historical David is dead (Ezek. 34.23-24). In this figure various aspects of leadership converge: anointing, kingship, Son of God, future hope. This emerging hope represents the clearest line of messianic expectation within the Old Testament.

Expectation of a Davidic king over Israel is heightened in the writings of pre-Christian Judaism. The *Psalms of Solomon*, dated between 70–45 BCE, give clearest expression to this understanding of kingship. Yahweh is the eternal king who reigns over Israel and the nations (*Pss. Sol.* 17.1-3). This sovereignty is expressed through David, whom Yahweh chose as king over Israel (17.4). God has promised to extend David's kingdom forever through his descendants (17.4). Because of Israel's sin and the intervention of evil leaders (Hasmoneans?) and foreign enemies (Pompey?), the Davidic reign is broken (17.5-18a). Even nature has ceased to bless Israel (17.18b-20). The prayer of *Pss. Sol.* 17.21-32 represents the transformed hope for God's kingship:

> See, Lord, and raise up for them their king,
> the son of David, to rule over your servant Israel
> in the time known to you, O God (17.21).

The Davidic king is to purge Jerusalem of foreign rulers and of sinfulness (17.21-25). The psalmist prays that 'At his warning the nations will flee from his presence: and he will condemn sinners by the thoughts of their hearts' (17.25). The Davidic king will re-establish God's rule in righteousness (17.26-32). In this figure all of the ideals of God's kingship converge:

> And he will be a righteous king over them, taught by God,
> There shall be no unrighteousness among them in his days,
> for all shall be holy,
> and their king shall be the Lord Messiah (17.32).

Clearly the concept of king of Israel provides the point of origin for the central messianic developments of the Old Testament and pre-Christian Judaism. While messianic images remain largely unfocused within the Old Testament, sharper focus is reached in the last century BCE. Though messianic expectations remain diverse throughout this period, the image of the Davidic king provides one clear messianic figure. Various concepts are drawn into the orbit of this figure. The expected leader is Sprout of Jesse, Shoot of David, Son of David (Isa. 11.10; Jer. 23.5; 33.15; Zech. 3.8; 6.12; *Pss. Sol.* 17.21). He is God's Son (2 Sam. 7.14; Ps. 89.26-27), he is Israel's king (*Pss. Sol.* 17.21, 32), and he is the Lord Messiah (*Pss. Sol.* 17.32).[1]

The concept of a messianic king surfaces in the Christian Gospels, where it is a rather ambivalent title for Jesus (Mt. 2.2; 27.11, 29, 37; 27.42; Mk 15.2, 9, 12, 18, 26, 32; Lk. 23.3, 36-38; Jn 1.49; 12.13; 18.33, 37, 39; 19.3, 14-15, 19, 21). Hans Conzelmann notes the striking phenomenon that the oft-mentioned kingdom which Jesus proclaims is not connected to his status as king.[2] It is significant that Jesus is not described as King of the Jews or King of Israel in the New Testament outside of the Gospels. The Revelation establishes Christ as the end time king who will rule over the world. Little use was made of this title in the post-apostolic period. It is likely that the reality of Jesus' death and the complexities of Roman rule reduced the impact of this title within early Christianity. While messianic speculation endured, rabbinical Judaism exercised a similar caution in messianic use of the title King.

The Literary Foreground

The King title develops from its widespread use in the Old Testament into a clearly focused messianic image in the first century BCE. Within the literary world of the Gospel of Mark the title is given quite different treatment.

Distribution

The kingship title (βασιλεύς) is employed only within the span of Mk 15.1-32; there it is applied to Jesus six times (15.2, 9, 12, 18, 26, 32).

---

1. See the discussion of the textual evidence for this term, *OTP*, II, pp. 667-68.

2. H. Conzelmann, *An Outline of the Theology of the New Testament* (trans. J. Bowden; London: SCM Press, 1969 [1968]), p. 75.

The title is initially presented by Pilate in the form of a question: 'Are you the king of the Jews?' (15.2). The ambiguous reply of Jesus in 15.2 (σὺ λέγεις) is turned to silence in 15.5. In 15.9, 12, Pilate attaches the title explicitly to Jesus. Thus, the King title is first assigned to Jesus by a Roman authority through a triadic pattern of repetition.

This newly assigned title is reinforced through a threefold chorus in 15.18, 26, 32. First the soldiers (15.18), then the inscription (15.26), then the religious leaders (15.32) echo the title. As a result the King title is assigned to Jesus only within a narrow span of the narrative. The sixfold echoing of the title by various characters within this span creates a brief, singular focus on the idea of Jesus as King.

Association

The images associated with the King title are wholly negative. The title is first assigned by a Roman magistrate and is employed by him to bait the religious authorities (15.2, 9, 12). This taunting accusation is taken up and amplified by the violent mockery of the soldiers (15.18) and the sarcasm of the religious leaders (15.32). The leaders connect the term to the Christ title and seem to understand both in political terms (15.32). This image of the failed pretender to the throne of Israel is made public by the inscription (15.26). These associations produce a wholly negative aura around the title of King.

Confirmation

Nothing within the narrative affirms the King title. Jesus never employs the term, nor does he accept it as a proper description. The ambiguous reply of 15.3 is followed in 15.5 by absolute silence. No disciple or defender employs the title, and the narrator does nothing to salvage the term. Only the cry of the crowd in 11.9-10 suggests a positive association with kingship. Even this connection remains ambiguous and undeveloped. Consequently the King title remains a narrative taunt employed only by the opponents of Jesus and only in view of his approaching execution.

Development

The larger narrative reinforces and develops the negative images of the King title. Within the local context the oppressive traits of the image are demonstrated in the violent abuse carried out by the soldiers (15.16-20). Jesus is seated in the halls of power and garbed in the robes of political authority. This derisive passion play confirms the malevolence of the King title.

Within the larger narrative the King title is set against a backdrop of violence and abuse. Herod provides the model in 6.14, 22, 25, 26, 27. The kingship of Herod is played out explicitly against the death of John the Baptist. Thus, kingship and martyrdom are linked in the world of the narrative.

A similar image is put forth in Mk 13.9, where disciples are to bear a future witness before governors and kings. This age too is marked by martyrdom (13.12-13).

Consequently the connotations of the kingship title are wholly violent. In the past the Baptist died at the hands of the king. In the future disciples will again endure the violent judgment of kings. In the present Jesus stands mocked and condemned under the rubric of the kingship title.

Effect

The impact of this strategy is noteworthy. In the Gospel of Mark the King title is concentrated in a tight circle around the death of Jesus. Initiated by Pilate and echoed by soldiers and religious leaders, the King title embodies the violent rejection which leads to Jesus' death. The title is never embraced by Jesus, by his followers, nor by the narrator. The scenes in Mark 15 are played out against a larger pattern of kingly violence and judgment. The narrative strategy thus abandons the kingship imagery as an inadequate expression of Jesus' task and identity. The King title belongs instead to those who instigate violence, first against the Baptist, then against Jesus and his followers.

Conclusion

The historical and literary development of the King title illustrate the need for formalist narrative analysis alongside the history of the tradition. The king of Israel concept provides one of the few clearly-defined messianic titles from the pre-Christian era. Its origin and expansion within the political and spiritual development of Israel may be observed. The potential of the term is evident. The connection of this title to the reign of Yahweh in terms of anointing, agency and sonship preserves the monotheistic ethos of the Old Testament. The linkage to King David, based on scriptural proof, ensures the continuity of the tradition. The blending of political and spiritual tasks ensures its validity as a concept of renewal. As the Pharisaic prayers of the *Psalms of Solomon* demonstrate, the concept of the Davidic king gathered up vital strands of messianic hope within Israel.

Despite the inertia of this development, the Gospel of Mark presents the King title as an inappropriate name for Jesus. This pattern of rejection and reversal is certainly related to political and sociological factors, and it may emerge from the consciousness of Jesus. At the first level of observation, however, the refusal to name Jesus as King is a narrative construction. While the claim to kingship is not silenced in the characterization of Jesus, this claim is redefined in the Gospel of Mark as a taunting indictment brought by others. The title is ultimately attached to figures who practice violence and abuse. Jesus, like his predecessor and his followers, is among those who suffer at the hands of kings.

The formal strategy at work in the Gospel of Mark thus realigns and relocates the traditional development of the kingship imagery. The title can no longer provide a predetermined definition by which to evaluate the activity of Jesus; in the Gospel of Mark the fate of Jesus provides the pattern by which to judge—and eventually abandon—this oppressive image.

Chapter 7

THE TEACHER

> And they awake him and say to him, 'Teacher, does it not concern you
> that we are perishing?' (Mk 4.38).

The image of the teacher plays an important role within the Old Testament and Judaism, but only a small portion of this tradition is eschatological or messianic. Nonetheless the image of the teacher is central
to the characterization of Jesus in the Gospel of Mark.

The Historical Background

While the role of teacher is central to faith in the Old Testament, there
is no clear messianic expectation around this office. The Old Testament
portrays God as the end time teacher of Israel (Isa. 30.20; 51.4). This
eschatological instruction is an extension of Yahweh's continuing relationship to Israel (Isa. 48.17). This teaching tradition has connections to
the developing Wisdom concepts, and there may be overtones of a
messianic teaching in Isa. 11.1-2:

> A shoot shall come out from the stump of Jesse
> and a branch shall grow out of his roots.
> The spirit of the Lord shall rest upon him,
> the spirit of wisdom and understanding,
> the spirit of council and might,
> the spirit of knowledge and the fear of the Lord.

Beyond this the Old Testament has no clear and enduring conception
of a messianic teacher who will arise at the end time.

Attempts to find expectation of a messianic teacher within Judaism
meet with similar difficulties.[1] Most texts which deal with this imagery

---

1.   See the detailed attempt by Riesner, *Jesus als Lehrer*. Traces of a messianic
teacher have been sought in the following texts: CD 6.11; 7.18; 4QFlor 1.11;
11QMelch 18-20; *T. Jud.* (A)21.1-4; *T. Levi* 18.2-6; *Pss. Sol.* 17.42-43; 18.4-9; *1*

do not expect a messiah defined by his role as the teacher; rather they typically describe a traditional messiah whose activity is accompanied by Godly wisdom. This trait does little to distinguish this figure from a host of others within Judaism. Consequently most of Jewish expectation does not center on a messianic teacher, but on a messiah who, like others, teaches with wisdom. Thus, the priestly messiah of the Testament of the Twelve Patriarchs (*T. Levi* 18) will teach with wisdom. The Davidic messiah of the *Psalms of Solomon* is marked by wisdom, but his teaching activity is secondary to his political role (*Pss. Sol.* 17.21-46). In the targum on Isaiah 53 the messiah seems to provide instruction. While teaching will characterize the activity of the messiah, there is no clear messianic concept of a coming teacher.

The nearest model for such a figure lies in the Teacher of Righteousness from Qumran. He is clearly the end time teacher (1Q 4.22), and instruction forms an important part of the messianic gestalt at Qumran. Nonetheless, the Teacher is probably not a messianic figure at Qumran.[2] The two messiahs—priestly and political—are future figures who will follow upon the period of instruction by the Teacher of Righteousness. The Teacher of Righteousness is himself a historical figure who probably founded the settlement and died in the middle of its history. Ideas of the expectation of his return are vague.[3]

While much evidence is missing from the historical development, a coherent line emerges. Although teaching is a part of all of Israel's religion and God is Israel's true teacher, some conception of messianic instruction develops. Teaching with wisdom is a trait found in various types of messianic expectation, but there seems no clear conception of a messianic figure defined primarily in terms of his role as teacher.

A similar situation emerges in early Christianity. While the New Testament gives extensive witness to the central role of Jesus' teaching activity, the Teacher title played little part in the developing thought of the early Church.[4]

En. 46.3; 49.3-4; 51.3; *Memar marqa* 4.12; *Targ. Isa.* 53.5, 11; *Targ. Gen.* 49.10; *Midr. Ps.* 21.90a. See also M. Hengel, 'Jesus als messianischer Lehrer Weisheit und die Anfänge der Christologie', *Sagesse et Religion: Colloque de Strasbourg (octobre 1976)* (Bibliothèque d'Etudes Supérieures spécialisé d'Histoire des Religions de Strasbourg; Paris, 1979), pp. 147-88.

2.   J. Fitzmyer, *Responses to 101 Questions on the Dead Sea Scrolls* (New York: Paulist Press, 1992), p. 57.

3.   Fitzmyer, *Responses*, pp. 61-63.

4.   Donald Guthrie, *New Testament Theology* (Leicester: Inter-Varsity Press,

The Literary Foreground

Over against this background the Gospel of Mark employs the Teacher title and teaching imagery as a central component in its portrait of Jesus. While this imagery echoes various traditions within the Old Testament and Judaism and most certainly reflects the historical activity of Jesus, the characterization of Jesus as the messianic Teacher is a narrative construction sponsored by the designs of this Gospel.

Distribution

Twelve instances of the Teacher title (διδάσκαλος) are evenly distributed across the face of the narrative (4.38; 5.35; 9.17, 38; 10.17, 20, 35; 12.14, 19, 32; 13.1; 14.14). The title appears in a variety of settings. It is found in miracle stories (4.38; 5.35; 9.17), in theological discussion (9.17, 38; 10.17, 20, 35; 13.1), in debate scenes (12.4, 19, 32), and in the preparation for the Passover (14.14). Thus, the Teacher title provides a frequent and diverse image of Jesus.

Association

The narrative connects the Teacher title with distinct images of Jesus. Three major patterns of association are present.

First, the narrative creates an unexpected link between the Teacher title and Jesus' activity as wonder worker. The most dramatic example of this connection appears in Mk 4.38. In the dark of the night, in the midst of the sea, in the throes of a storm, the disciples awaken Jesus and call upon him to save them. Strangely, the address used in this hour of crisis is that of Teacher (διδάσκαλε). The narrative thus creates a link between Jesus' creative power to heal and save and his designation as the Teacher. In addition, wonder and amazement are attached to the Teacher title (4.41).

This unusual linkage is confirmed by the scene in Mk 5.21-43. Two stories of healing are presented. The healing of the woman (5.25-34) is inserted into the healing of the ruler's daughter (5.21-24, 35-43). Various narrative elements link the two stories. In the midst of this healing complex, Jesus is designated as διδάσκαλος, the Teacher (5.35). This

1981), pp. 269-70, employs the reasoning of O. Cullmann on the role of the prophet title to conclude that 'the concept of prophet (as also teacher) plays no significant part in NT Christology' (p. 270).

strategy reinforces the connection between Jesus' creative power and his role as the Teacher.

The linkage is confirmed by the Capernaum scene of Mk 1.21-29. Three miracle stories (1.23-28; 1.29-31; 1.32-34) provide clear demonstration of Jesus' teaching with authority (1.21-22).[5]

A second line of association is found in the narrative link between the debate and controversy which surrounds Jesus and his designation as the Teacher. A number of stories center around theological discussions with little or no controversy. In Mk 9.38-40 the question of other disciples is raised. Jesus insists that 'whoever is not against us is for us' (9.40). In 10.17-22 a rich man inquires about eternal life. Jesus insists upon the exclusive goodness of God (10.18) and demands obedience to the commandments of God (10.19). The final demand of Jesus is radical: 'Go sell what you have and give to the poor... and come follow me' (10.21). In Mk 10.35-40 Jesus is called upon to grant power to the sons of Zebedee. Jesus instructs the power-hungry disciples about his cup and his baptism (10.38). In ch. 13 the observation by the disciples initiates Jesus' eschatological discourse about the Temple. Each of these discussions designates Jesus as the Teacher (9.38; 10.17, 35; 13.1).

A more dramatic connection is found in scenes of controversy. In Mk 12.13-17 Jesus is confronted by representatives of the Pharisees and the Herodians. These groups have been shown plotting Jesus' death in Mk 3.6. Here their questions are designed to trap Jesus (12.13). Following a flattering preface (12.14), they pose to Jesus a double-edged question: 'Is it lawful to give tribute to Caesar or not? Should we give or not give?' (12.14). The answer of Jesus is equally double-edged: 'The things of Caesar give to Caesar, but those of God to God' (12.17).

A second controversy follows in 12.18-27. Here a Sadducee questions Jesus on the issue of marriage and death. Behind the question lies a challenge to belief in the resurrection (12.23). Jesus addresses both questions, concluding with a declaration that 'God is not of the dead, but the living' (12.27).

The debate in 12.28-34 centers around the primary commandment (12.28). Jesus cites the Shema of Deut. 6.4-5 and the love command of Lev. 19.18. The scribe affirms the answer of Jesus (12.32-33) and is told that he is 'not far from the kingdom of God' (12.34).

---

5.   On this connection see Broadhead, *Teaching with Authority*, pp. 56-71.

Significantly, all three scenes belong to the context of Jesus' temple debates (11.27) and are addressed to religious authorities. In each scene Jesus is addressed as the Teacher (12.14, 19, 32). While the first two scenes embody rejection of Jesus' teaching, the third scene leaves open the response of the scribe.

As a consequence the Gospel of Mark connects the Teacher title to two images: the wondrous creative power of Jesus and the authority of Jesus in debate. These two lines are united in Mk 9.14-29. The healing focus appears in 9.20-27 when Jesus drives out the evil spirit and heals the boy. The controversy theme is found both in 9.14, where Jesus argues with the disciples, and in the failure of the disciples to heal the boy (9.17-18, 28-29). At the center of this account stands the address of Jesus as the Teacher (9.17).

A third pattern of association may be observed. Jesus' teaching with authority and his controversy with the leaders of Israel lead eventually to the passion story. The charge of blasphemy and the death plot both originate in controversial miracle scenes (2.7; 3.6). The final death plot emerges precisely in response to Jesus' teaching (12.12). As a consequence the activity of Jesus as the Teacher stands in close association with his suffering and death.

Confirmation
The narrative strategy wholly confirms the image of Jesus as the Teacher. The crowds are amazed at his teaching (1.32), and they hear him gladly (12.37). The teaching of Jesus carries an authority which distinguishes him from the scribes (1.22). His teaching is marked by creative healing power (9.17). The instructions of the Teacher guide the way of discipleship (9.38-40; 10.17-22, 35-40; 13.1-37). His words interpret the Scriptures of the Old Testament and reveal the will of God (12.13-17, 18-27, 28-34). He is able to pose riddles (12.35-37), to answer the unanswerable question (12.13-17), and to silence all debate (12.34). The Teacher is able to draw willing inquirers near to the kingdom of God (12.34). Through various techniques and connections the narrative demonstrates the creative, healing, instructive power of Jesus and thus confirms the Teacher title.

Development
The Gospel of Mark creates a stark and complex image of Jesus through its development of the Teacher title. The miracle stories confirm the authority of Jesus' teaching. The activity of the Teacher stands at the

center of the controversy with the religious leaders. This controversy flows eventually into the passion narrative. Beyond this, the image is given narrative depth and extension through passages which demonstrate Jesus' teaching, but do so without using the title.

Various passages refer to the substance of Jesus' teaching. The διδαχή of Jesus is noted in Mk 1.22, 27; 4.2; 11.18; 12.38. In 1.22,27 διδαχή refers to the manner of Jesus' teaching and to the authority it bears. In Mk 4.2 and 12.38 the focus falls on the content of his teaching: Mk 4.3-9 contains a parable, while 12.38-40 contains a warning. The amazement of the people in 11.18 seems to focus both the manner and the content of Jesus' instruction.

More frequently, the Gospel of Mark focuses the activity of Jesus' instruction. Numerous passages highlight the activity of Jesus as a teacher (1.21, 22; 2.13; 4.1, 2; 6.2, 6, 30, 34; 7.7; 8.31; 9.31; 10.1; 11.17; 12.14, 35; 14.49). This strategy gives complex narrative depth and detail to the Teacher title.

Mark 1.21, 22 create a decisive backdrop for the ministry of Jesus. Mark 1.21-39 presents the initial day of Jesus' ministry through his activity in Capernaum. This opening day serves as a paradigm for the work of Jesus throughout Galilee (1.38-39). The Capernaum model centers around three miracle scenes: an exorcism (1.21-28), a healing (1.29-31) and a summary scene of healing (1.32-35). Significantly, the narrative frames these stories and describes them as typical of Jesus' ministry of proclamation (1.21, 38-39). The narrative thus employs Jesus' wonders to demonstrate the authority of his teaching. This unusual and unexpected connection realigns the parameters of both the Teacher title and the miracle worker imagery.[6]

This connection is confirmed in Mk 6.34-44. While this scene centers around a feeding miracle, the primary theme is didactic. When Jesus sees the people as 'sheep without a shepherd' (Mk 6.34/Num. 27.17), he responds by teaching them. Thus, the association of Jesus' instruction with his miracle activity further interprets the Teacher title.

Jesus' teaching activity is linked to his relationship with the crowds in various scenes. In 2.13 and in 4.1, 2 Jesus teaches the crowds beside the sea. Both scenes are tied to images of discipleship (2.14; 4.3-34). The people are amazed at his teaching in 1.21-22 and in 6.2.

---

6. This pattern is fully described in Broadhead, *Teaching with Authority*, pp. 56-71.

Jesus' teaching activity is closely associated with his call to discipleship. Discipleship images follow various teaching scenes (2.13-14; 4.1, 2; 8.31; 9.31). In 2.14 Jesus calls Levi to follow him. In 4.3-34 Jesus instructs his disciples in a series of parables. Following two of his passion instructions (8.31; 9.31), Jesus gives a lesson on discipleship (8.34-38; 9.33-50).[7] In 6.30 the disciples report to Jesus their own teaching ministry.

Important scenes link Jesus' teaching activity to opposition from religious leaders and to the role of the temple. Mark 7.6-7 cites Isa. 29.13 to contrast the teaching of the Pharisees and the Jerusalem leaders—who teach human teaching—with that of Jesus. This opposition is further developed around the image of the Temple. In 11.15-19 Jesus cleanses the Temple, then teaches (11.17) from the Old Testament. The teaching activity (11.15-16) and teaching content (11.17) both focus on Temple worship. This teaching is heard by chief priests and scribes, who then plot his death (11.18).

A similar scene is found in Mk 12.13-17. Pharisees and Herodians seek to flatter Jesus with the compliment that he 'is teaching the way of God in truth' (12.14). Jesus knows their hypocrisy (12.15) and asks 'Why do you tempt me?' (12.15). The larger context of this exchange is the Temple debates (11.27).

This context is made clear in Mk 12.35-44, where Jesus himself takes the initiative to teach (12.35). His instruction addresses the activity of the scribes (12.35, 38) and the wealthy (12.41). The scene of this instruction is Jesus' teaching in the Temple (12.35).

This tie between teaching, opponents and Temple is given dramatic confirmation in Mk 14.49. In the face of his arrest, Jesus declares that 'through the days I was with you in the Temple teaching and you did not seize me'.

Jesus' rejection and passion are linked closely to his teaching activity. In the synagogue of his hometown (6.1-6) Jesus finds amazement (6.2), questions (6.2-3) and unbelief (6.6). This rejection is closely linked to his teaching (6.2, 6). Mark 8.31 and 9.31 speak of the Son of Man in terms of his destiny of suffering, death and resurrection. Both passages are defined in terms of Jesus' teaching activity. The charge of

---

7.   The passion saying in 10.32-34 is followed by both the διδάσκαλος title and by instruction in discipleship (10.35-45).

blasphemy and the death plot originate in controversial scenes demonstrating the authority of Jesus' teaching (2.7; 3.6). The death plot unfolds in response to Jesus' teaching (12.12).

Four key summary passages gather the entirety of Jesus' ministry under the framework of teaching activity. The scene in Mk 1.21-39 serves as a paradigm for Jesus' ministry in Galilee and beyond.[8] The framework of this story defines this miracle activity in terms of proclamation—teaching and preaching (1.22, 39). Thus, Jesus' teaching with authority (1.22) defines the nature of his itinerant ministry.

This pattern is echoed in Mk 6.1-6. Following his rejection in his hometown, Jesus begins an itinerant teaching ministry in the surrounding villages (6.6).

Jesus eventually brings this work to Judea. Leaving Capernaum (9.33), Jesus crosses the Jordan and is met by the crowds (10.1). There Jesus again practices his teaching ministry. This act is turned into a generalizing summary statement through two elements: the use of an inceptive imperfect (ἐδίδασκεν) and the note that this is a standing custom of Jesus (εἰώθει in the pluperfect).

The teaching ministry of Jesus extends finally into the Jerusalem story. While various scenes show teaching activity in and around Jerusalem (11.17; 12.14, 35), the summary in 14.49 places the whole of the Jerusalem ministry under the teaching framework: 'Through the days I was before you in the Temple, teaching.'

These four scenes highlight the teaching activity of Jesus at crucial junctures of his ministry: the opening day in Capernaum (1.21-22), the ministry around Galilee (6.6), the activity in Judea (10.1), the final days in Jerusalem (14.49). In addition, these summaries produce a generalizing effect which casts the entire work of Jesus under the framework of his teaching activity.

The διδάσκαλος title is further developed through the parallel title of Rabbi—ῥαββί and ῥαββουνί. While linguistically and historically ῥαββί and ῥαββουνί belong to the same stream of thought, they operate as separate elements within the world of the narrative. In the Gospel of Mark, ῥαββί appears in 9.5; 11.21; 14.45 and ῥαββουνί in 10.51.

The title ῥαββί is associated in each instance with failed discipleship. In Mk 9.5 Peter inappropriately responds to the transfiguration event: 'Rabbi, it is good for us to be here. Indeed, let us build three tabernacles.' The narrator confirms Peter's failure: 'For he did not know

8. See Broadhead, *Teaching with Authority*, pp. 56-71.

what he should answer, for he was terrified' (9.6). The heavenly voice directs the focus instead to the Beloved Son and to his passion teachings (9.7).

A similar failure to understand is found in Peter's address of Jesus as Rabbi in Mk 11.12-26. The enigmatic cursing of the fig tree (11.12-14) is clarified by the enclosed Temple scene (11.15-19). Peter's response seemingly fails to comprehend this connection, and Jesus instructs his followers on faith, prayer and forgiveness (11.22-26).

The Rabbi title points to a different type of failure in Mk 14.43-52. Judas betrays Jesus with a kiss and with a single word of address: ῥαββί. Jesus is abandoned by his other followers as well: one resorts to the sword (14.47), and all flee (14.50-52).

As a consequence the ῥαββί title is associated exclusively with failed discipleship. Peter represents the whole group in his failure to comprehend. This discipleship failure theme is widely developed in the Gospel of Mark and is focused uniquely around the ῥαββί title.

In contrast, the alternate form of ῥαββουνί embodies a positive model of discipleship. This title appears only in 10.51 in the story of Bartimaeus. 'What do you want me to do for you?' is a standard question posed by Jesus (10.36, 51). In response to this question James and John ask for positions of power and glory (10.37)—a stark contradiction to the way of service and discipleship (10.45). In contrast, Bartimaeus responds with a plea for sight (10.51) and with discipleship along the way to the cross (10.52). The insistent Bartimaeus thus becomes a model for following Jesus. This model is associated with his address of Jesus as ῥαββουνί (10.51).

Thus, use of the Rabbi title is preserved wholly for the issue of discipleship. Two stark images mark those who address Jesus as Rabbi. Peter and the Twelve fail to understand Jesus, one betrays him, and all forsake him. In contrast, Bartimaeus insists upon the gift of sight, then uses it to follow Jesus in the way.

Effect

The effect of this narrative construction is significant. Within the Gospel of Mark the title of Teacher stands at the summit of a complex christological strategy. The διδάσκαλος (Teacher) title is used explicitly on 12 occasions. These are evenly distributed across the·narrative and occur in a variety of settings. This title is associated with the creative power present in Jesus' wonders and with the authority of Jesus in debate and controversy. These lead ultimately to his passion. The narrative employs various techniques to confirm the positive status of the διδάσκαλος title.

This didactic Christology is also developed through scenes and structures which employ the imagery of the Teacher, but not the title. Substantive reference to Jesus' instruction (διδαχή) focuses both the manner and content of Jesus' teaching. More attention is given to the activity of the Teacher. The authority of Jesus' teaching is demonstrated in miracle scenes. His teaching activity guides his relation with the crowds and develops his call to discipleship. Opposition from religious authorities and against the Temple centers around the teaching of Jesus. Jesus' rejection and his death are tied closely to his teaching activity. Four key summaries (1.22; 6.6; 10.1; 14.49) focus teaching activity at the crucial junctures of Jesus' ministry and place the whole of his life under the framework of his teaching. The Hebrew form of the Teacher title is used to generate true and false models of discipleship. As a consequence the Teacher title and the larger teaching imagery play a crucial role in the characterization of Jesus.

Conclusion

The portrayal of Jesus as the Teacher in the Gospel of Mark illustrates key aspects in the process of naming Jesus. First, this image demonstrates that narrative descriptions can never be fully elucidated through external factors. The history and background of the Teacher title fail to illuminate its vital role in the portrait of Jesus. Consequently critical scholarship and confessing Christianity have given far too little attention to this description of Jesus. While elements such as the Teacher imagery have important connections in the history of the tradition and in the consciousness of Jesus, they now operate under the strategic guidance of narrative frameworks. As this study demonstrates, one important key to interpretation lies in the patterns of the narrative worlds which host these images.

Secondly, these potent narrative descriptions cannot be reduced to a catalogue of terms and titles. Oft-repeated titles may prove ambiguous, while sharply focused descriptions may be built around seldom-spoken titles. We must look for narrative images rather than linguistic terms alone, and we must weigh rather than count them. The characterization of Jesus is ultimately more than a collection of data; it is a performance. This is particularly true of the Teacher image.

Finally, narratives create significance not only by *what* they say, but more so by *how* they say. The narrative whole proves greater than the sum of its part. Content, structure and strategy combine to articulate complex and carefully-nuanced narrative descriptions.

The description of Jesus as the Teacher in the Gospel of Mark exemplifies this process and illustrates the need for formalist narrative analysis alongside the history of the traditions. Over against a divergent and unfocused background and standing in stark contrast to the reticence of the early Church, the Teacher image emerges in the Gospel of Mark as a decisive, clearly focused description of Jesus.

Chapter 8

SHEPHERD

I will strike the shepherd, and the sheep will be scattered (Zech. 13.7;
Mk 14.27).

The shepherd imagery has a diverse background in the Old Testament.
Some strands of this traditon are connected to messianic expectations,
and this link is developed in various areas of the New Testament.

The Historical Background

The Shepherd title and shepherd imagery have varied use in the Old
Testament. (1) The image refers often to literal keepers of sheep (Gen.
29.3; Num. 14.33; Amos 1.1), and various metaphors are built upon
this image (Isa. 40.11; Ps. 49.14). (2) Israel is refered to as God's flock
and those who lead Israel as shepherds (1 Kgs 22.17; 2 Chron. 18.16).
(3) The leaders of Israel in general are called shepherds (Jer. 3.15; 23.1-
4; Ezek. 34.2; 1 Chron. 17.6). (4) David is known both as a literal shepherd and as the shepherd of Israel (Ps. 78.70-72; 2 Sam. 5.2; 1 Chron.
11.2). (5) Cyrus is described as God's shepherd (Isa. 44.28). (6) The
term is used of unidentified leaders (Zech. 13.7-9; Eccl. 12.11). (7) The
title is applied to the prophet or to the prophetic task (Zech. 11.4), and
it is used of false prophets as well (Jer. 10.21; 23.1). (8) The Shepherd
title and imagery are used of Yahweh in relation to Israel (Gen. 49.24;
Pss. 23.1; 28.9; 80.1; Isa. 40.11; Ezek. 34.15; Mic. 7.14). (9) The shepherd image is applied to a coming Davidic leader, thus taking on messianic overtones, in Ezek. 34.23-24:

> I will set up over them one shepherd, my servant David, and he shall
>   feed them:
> he shall feed them and be their shepherd.
> And I, the Lord, will be their God,
> and my servant David shall be prince among them;
> I, the Lord, have spoken.

The messianic shepherd imagery is projected back upon the Old Testament era in *4 Ezra*, a Christian writing from around 100 CE:

> I, Ezra, received a command from the Lord on Mount Horeb to go to Israel. When I came to them they rejected me and refused the Lord's commandment. Therefore I say to you, O nations that hear and understand, Await for your shepherd; he will give you everlasting rest, because he who will come at the end of the age is close at hand. Be ready for the rewards of the kingdom, because the eternal light will shine upon you forevermore (*4 Ezra* 2.33-36).

Thus, shepherding becomes in the Old Testament a primary metaphor for God's care over Israel. This care is carried out through a host of agents—judges, prophets, Cyrus, David. The primary human shepherd of the Old Testament is David, probably because of his vocation. Because David is God's shepherd over Israel, the connection to messianic images lies close at hand. The figure whom God will raise up to lead Israel is to be a Davidic king (Jer. 23.5-6). Like David, this messianic figure is seen as the shepherd over Israel in Ezek. 34.23-24.

The image of the messiah as God's shepherd is picked up at scattered places in the New Testament. In the Fourth Gospel, Jesus is the Good Shepherd who gives his life for the flock (Jn 10.2, 11, 12, 14, 16). Jesus is the Great Shepherd in Heb. 13.20. The Lamb will be the shepherd of the people in Rev. 7.17. 1 Peter 2.25 calls Jesus the 'shepherd and guardian of your souls', and he is the Chief Shepherd (ἀρχιποίμην) in 1 Pet. 5.4. Thus, early Christianity described the pastoral activity of Jesus over the Church in the images of the shepherd and the flock.

The Literary Foreground

The shepherd image appears at two places in the Gospel of Mark, both of which are Old Testament citations. Mark 6.34 cites Num. 27.17 and similar passages to speak of the shepherdless people. Mark 14.27 cites Zech. 13.7 and tells of the striking of the shepherd and the scattering of the flock. In each case the shepherd concept is linked only indirectly to Jesus and his activity.

The Gospel of Mark associates three important concepts with the image of Jesus as God's shepherd to Israel. The first arises in the middle of a miracle story in Mk 6.32-46. Jesus sees the gathering crowd in Old Testament images as 'sheep not having a shepherd' (Mk 6.34; Num. 27.17; 1 Kgs 22.17; 2 Chron. 18.16). Jesus addresses the need of the people in two ways: he first teaches them (Mk 6.34), then he feeds

them (6.41-44). This pastoral image may be extended by the notice that
Jesus remains behind to send the people on their way (6.45-46). Thus,
this miracle story presents Jesus as a shepherd who cares for the flock
of God. Various elements within the scene extend this image. Beyond
the citation in Mk 6.34, the mention of green grass (χλωρῷ χόρτῳ) in
6.39 extends the shepherd imagery through reference to Psalm 23. The
use of the number 12 may allude to the tribes of Israel. The Old Testament portrait of Israel is most clearly recalled in the feeding in a
desert place (6.32, 35): this recalls the feeding of the children of Israel
in the wilderness. In so doing the theological milieu of the Exodus is
transported into the feeding story. Mark 6.32-46 thus becomes the story
of the calling and nurturing of a shepherdless people that is to become
the people of God. This Jewish image is replicated in a Gentile setting
in Mk 8.1-10.[1]

This imagery contains both characterization and critique. Because
this shepherd imagery draws upon Old Testament images, the metaphor
of Israel as God's flock is appropriated. The scene thus points to the
failed leadership which has left the people of God abandoned and in
danger—a common theme in the prophets (Jer. 10.21; 12.10; 50.6;
Ezek. 34.2, 5, 8). Over against this critique stands the positive characterization of Jesus. In view of the failure of the leaders of Israel, Jesus
shepherds the scattered flock of God. He does so first of all through his
instruction, then through the gift of food.

Thus, the Gospel of Mark employs shepherd imagery reflective of the
Old Testament in order to characterize Jesus. Most of the later New
Testament images of Jesus as a shepherd echo this pastoral image of
Jesus as one who cares for the people of God (Jn 10.2, 11, 12, 14, 16;
Heb. 13.30; 1 Pet. 2.25).

The second line of development associates shepherd imagery with
the death of Jesus. The striking down of the shepherd represents contrasting images in the Old Testament. In some instances false shepherds
are removed by God (Ezek. 34.10; see also Jer. 51.23). In the vision of
Micaiah, God will strike down King Ahab and leave Israel scattered on
the mountains, like sheep that have no shepherd (1 Kgs 22.13-38). In
Jer. 51.23 Yahweh gives the warrior strength to smash shepherds and
their flocks.

This image prevails in Zechariah 13. Yahweh will establish a foun-
tain of forgiveness in the house of David (13.1). Yahweh will remove

---

1.   See Broadhead, *Teaching with Authority*, pp. 117-23; 137-39.

idols, false prophets and unclean spirits from the land (13.2-6). This purge is further described in shepherd imagery:

Awake, O sword, against my shepherd
against the man who is my associate,
says the Lord of hosts,
Strike the shepherd, that the sheep may be scattered;
I will turn my hand against the little ones (Zech. 13.7).

The outcome of this purge is a renewed people of God. One-third of the people will remain (13.8), and this third will be refined by fire (13.9). The result will be a new covenant relationship with Yahweh:

They will call on my name, and I will answer them.
I will say, 'They are my people';
and they will say, 'The Lord is our God' (Zech. 13.9).

There appears to be no instance in which an opponent strikes down God's shepherd and scatters the flock.

Mark 14.27 draws directly upon this Old Testament image of the shepherd who has been struck down. The citation from Zech. 13.7 affirms that it is Yahweh who strikes the shepherd—an idea not foreign to New Testament views of the death of Jesus. Nonetheless, the Gospel of Mark has set the Old Testament citation in a new context. The death of Jesus is linked clearly in this Gospel to his controversy with religious leaders (3.6; 6.6; 11.18). The focus in Mk 14.27 is not upon who strikes down Jesus, but upon the response of the disciples to this event. Jesus predicts that his followers will be scandalized by his death (14.27)—a point which Peter debates with vigor (14.29-31). The effect of this scene is that Jesus is characterized as the smitten and abandoned Shepherd. This characterization, constructed awkwardly from the Old Testament citation, forms a coherent part of the passion story in the Gospel of Mark.

A third character trait is sketched around the shepherd imagery. Having associated this image with Jesus in the feeding story of Mk 6.32-46 and the citation in view of Jesus' death (14.27), the narrative confirms a further aspect of the shepherd imagery. Following close upon the citation of Zech. 13.7 comes Jesus' prophecy that 'after I have been raised I will go before you into Galilee' (Mk 14.28). This connection characterizes Jesus as the Risen One who will reconstitute the flock of God in the wake of this tragedy. This image represents a further development of the Zechariah prophecy. As in ancient Israel, a purified remnant will be re-established as the people of God. The raising up of a Davidic shepherd (Ezek. 34.23-24) also echoes through this claim. This characterization is established in Mk 14.28 and confirmed in the door of the empty tomb: 'Go and say to his disciples and to Peter that he is going before you into Galilee. There you will see him, even as he said to you' (Mk 16.7).

Conclusion

The Gospel of Mark employs the image of the shepherd to characterize Jesus. This is accomplished without using the title explicitly of Jesus and with some contradiction to the Old Testament pattern. Building upon a general motif from the Old Testament, Jesus is described as the Shepherd who nurtures the scattered people of God, first of all through his instruction. The image of the smitten shepherd is applied to Jesus in the context of his death, but the focus falls primarily on the scattering of his followers. Jesus is finally sketched as the Shepherd who is raised up to gather and renew the scattered flock. In this way the Gospel of Mark takes scattered images from Old Testament tradition and employs them in subtle ways to name and characterize Jesus. This portrait is ultimately a narrative construct forged through the patterns and transitions of this Gospel.

Chapter 9

THE HOLY ONE OF GOD

And immediately there was in their synagogue a person in an unclean
spirit, and it cried saying, 'What to me and to you Jesus Nazarene. You
have come to destroy us. We know who you are—the Holy One of God'
(Mk 1.23-24).

Jesus is addressed in Mk 1.24 as ὁ ἅγιος τοῦ θεοῦ, the Holy One of
God. Both the origin of this term and its christological significance
prove difficult to establish.

The Historical Background

Various attempts have been made to establish a background for this description. A number of scholars see here a word-play based on the
transition from ναζιραῖον to the term ἅγιον θεοῦ in Judg. 13.7 and a
similar transition in Judg. 16.17. F. Mussner argues for an Aramaic
base behind this word-play,[1] though R. Pesch believes the word-play is
a community interpretation of the Nazarene designation, regardless of
the Aramaic behind the expression.[2] Others have attempted to connect
the term to Ps. 106.16, where Aaron is called 'the holy one of the
Lord', and to see Jesus as the messianic high priest.[3] The synagogue
exorcism in Mk 1.24 hardly expresses such imagery. The title also carries implications of a charismatic wonder worker.[4] The connection to
the Nazarite imagery would evoke a consecration similar to that of
Samuel or Samson (Judg. 13.7; 16.17; 1 Sam. 1.11). The Holy One of
God title appears only here in the synoptics and in Jn 6.69. The most

1. F. Mussner, 'Ein Wortspiel in Mk 1,24?', *BZ* NF 4 (1960), pp. 285-86.
2. Pesch, *Das Markusevangelium*, I, p. 122.
3. See, for example, Kertelge, *Die Wunder Jesu*, p. 53.
4. So H. Braun, *Qumran und das Neue Testament* (2 vols.; Tübingen: J.C.B.
Mohr [Paul Siebeck], 1966), I, p. 62; Hahn, *Titles*, pp. 231-35.

accurate evaluation of the background of the term is probably that of
J. Fitzmyer: 'It is unknown outside the NT.'[5] Consequently the title
reflects no real messianic background, but evokes a general image of
one who belongs uniquely to God.

The Literary Foreground

Over against this ambiguous background, the Holy One of God title has
a unique place in the Gospel of Mark. This distinctive role draws upon
the formal structures and strategies at work within this narrative.

Association

While this term is used only once in the Gospel of Mark (1.24), it is
associated with a central christological image: Jesus is an exorcist without equal. The exorcism pattern established in Mk 1.23-28 is oft-
repeated (Mk 1.21-29; 1.34; 1.39; 3.7-13; 5.1-21a; 7.24-31). Beyond
this, the language and imagery of exorcism emerge in other forms of
wonder stories (Mk 4.35–5.1). The Gospel of Mark, at first glance,
seems to employ 'the Holy One of God' to refer to the charismatic
power of Jesus expressed in his frequent exorcism of demons.

Confirmation

On the other hand, the Gospel of Mark does not repeat this description
and does nothing to directly confirm this title. While the command to
silence (Mk 1.25) serves the warfare at work within this story, it also
plays a role in the larger secrecy motif developed within the Gospel of
Mark. Within this narrative the identity of Jesus cannot be properly
understood through shrieking demons (1.25; 3.12) or misguided disciples (8.30; 9.9).

Development

The potential inherent in the image of Jesus as the Holy One of God is
not unleashed. Rather than exploiting the identity of Jesus as a demonstrative *Wundermann*, the power of Jesus over the demonic is developed through three distinct techniques.

First, the authority of Jesus over the demonic reflects more than an
individual charisma; it demonstrates the cosmic battle which God is
waging against satanic forces. Jesus is driven by the Spirit to wage

5.   Fitzmyer, *Luke*, p. 546.

warfare in the desert with Satan (Mk 1.12-13). This struggle is sand-wiched between the baptism and anointing of Jesus (1.9-11) and the announcement of the kingdom of God (1.14-15). Jesus' struggle with the demonic marks the end of the evil kingdom (3.23-27). Thus, the activity of Jesus cannot be interpreted simply in the light of previous charismatic figures, for it marks God's cosmic, eschatological warfare against the hosts of evil.

Secondly, the Gospel of Mark realigns the exorcisms and other mira-cles through a unique strategy of characterization.[6] The miracle activity in 1.21-39 is defined prospectively as 'teaching with authority'. Retro-spectively this activity is described as 'preaching' (1.38). Beyond this frame, the story itself understands the exorcism as an example of Jesus' teaching: 'What is this—a new teaching with authority?' (1.27). Mark 1.21-38 invokes this teaching imagery and imposes it upon the heal-ing in 1.39-45. This unusual connection is confirmed when Jesus is described as Teacher in the middle of miracle stories (4.38; 5.35; 6.34). In addition, the Gospel of Mark establishes a causal link between the miracles of Jesus and his passion. Jesus' miracle activity demonstrates the power of his teaching, and it is this teaching which leads to his death. Jesus is first accused of blasphemy within a miracle story (2.7). Subsequently the death plot against Jesus arises in response to his won-drous deeds (3.7). Both the charge of blasphemy and the death plot emerge anew in Jerusalem near the end of Jesus' life (14.64; 11.18). Whatever the historical basis for such a portrait, the narrative logic is clear: the authority of Jesus' instruction, which is demonstrated in his wondrous deeds, generates the ongoing controversy which leads to his death. In this way the narrative strategy overcomes the potential di-chotomy between the power of Jesus' deeds and the scandal of his death. Thus, the miracle activity has been taken up within the Gospel of Mark into a larger christological strategy which culminates in the death of Jesus.

Thirdly, the acclamation of Jesus as the Holy One of God is silenced through a command of Jesus (1.25), and it is never repeated in the Gospel of Mark. While this silencing is a typical motif in miracle stories,[7] the Gospel of Mark employs a larger pattern of secrecy around the identity of Jesus.

---

6. This strategy is sketched in detail in Broadhead, *Teaching with Authority*.

7. The naming of an opponent and the rebuke to silence represent attempts to exercise control over the opponent. See Luz, 'Das Geheimnismotiv', pp. 9-30.

Effect

The effect of this strategy is significant. The Holy One of God title is not directly confirmed, and no ongoing connection with the miracles of Jesus is established. Jesus' wonders serve instead to demonstrate his cosmic, eschatological battle with the forces of evil and to establish the core of his identity as the wondrous proclaimer who gives his life in the cause of God. This unique combination of power and suffering reflects the larger christological strategy of this Gospel.[8]

Conclusion

The Holy One of God presents a singular description of Jesus which has no real background. It acquires some degree of significance through the structures and strategies of the Gospel of Mark. Used only once, the title is associated with the image of Jesus as a charismatic exorcist, yet this association is not developed. The title is locked away under a command to silence, then the narrative develops the miracle stories along different lines. Exorcisms and other miracles serve in the Gospel of Mark to demonstrate the ultimate warfare which God is waging against satanic powers. More importantly, the miracle activity of Jesus demonstrates the authority of his teaching and flows into the story of his death. These patterns of narrative construction are unique. Ultimately this image is significant for what is *not* done with it: the title is not omitted, but it is also not developed. Consequently the Holy One of God remains an isolated and largely inconsequential description.

---

8.   This pattern is demonstrated in detail in Broadhead, *Prophet, Son, Messiah*.

Chapter 10

THE SUFFERING SERVANT OF GOD

> For even the Son of Man did not come to be served, but to serve and to give his life a ransom for the many (Mk 10.45).

The Servant of God title (παῖς θεοῦ) has a wide-ranging but ambiguous background in the Old Testament and Judaism. Its role in the New Testament and early Christianity is equally enigmatic.

The Historical Background

The Hebrew term for servant (*'ebed*) carries a variety of meanings within the Old Testament. At the profane level it may refer to a slave, to one who serves a king, to political submission, to a self-description marked by humility, or to servants in the sanctuary.[1] Its religious uses include its employment as a self-description of humility in the presence of God, as a plural form designating the pious, as a title for distinguished persons, and as the Suffering Servant of Deutero-Isaiah.[2] This term is most often translated in the Septuagint by παῖς or by δοῦλος.

The most significant aspect of this title is its relation to the Servant Hymns of Deutero-Isaiah (Isa. 42.1-4; 49.1-7; 50.4-11; 52.13–53.12). This title is applied in a collective way to Israel as a whole (Isa. 49.3). Other references seem to have an individual in mind (52.13–53.12).

A key issue in the background of this term is its use within Judaism around the New Testament era. The plural form (παῖδες θεοῦ) was used within Judaism to speak of Israel as the children of God (Wis. 9.4; 12.7, 20; 19.6). In a few instances the singular is also used in this way (Wis. 2.13; possibly Bar. 3.36). More frequent is the use of the singular παῖς θεοῦ to mean servant of God. Moses, the prophets, and the three

---

1. W. Zimmerli and J. Jeremias, *The Servant of God* (London: SCM Press, 1957 [1952]), pp. 9-13.
2. Zimmerli and Jeremias, *The Servant of God*, pp. 13-34.

men in the fiery furnace are described by this term. Joachim Jeremias contends that this use of Servant of God in Judaism carried forward the various meanings already found in the Old Testament.[3]

Was there a clear messianic understanding of this title within Judaism? In a number of passages God refers to the messiah as 'my servant' (Ezek. 34.32-33; 37.24-25; Zech. 3.8; *4 Ezra* 7.28; 13.32, 37, 52; 14.9; *2 Bar.* 70.9; *Targ. Isa.* 42.1; 43.10; 52.13; *Targ. Zech.* 3.8; *Targ. Ezek.* 34.23-24; 37.24-25). The most explicit connection is established in *2 Bar.* 70.9 and in the targum on Isaiah, both of which speak of 'my servant, the Messiah'. The remainder of rabbinic literature does not connect the idea of the messiah to the servant of God title.

Joachim Jeremias concludes that while Hellenistic Judaism 'is inclined to understand the παῖς θεοῦ of Deutero-Isaiah as "child of God" and prefers the collective interpretation',[4] the situation is quite different within Palestinian Judaism. Here he finds three lines of application: the collective interpretation, application to the prophet Isaiah, and messianic exegesis.[5] Citing various passages from this period of Judaism, Jeremias concludes that 'Messianic interpretations of certain Deut. Isa. passages can be most probably traced back to pre-Christian times'.[6] He further concludes that the texts interpreted messianically within Palestinian Judaism (Isa. 42.1-4, 6; 49.6; 52.13–53.12) were the same texts so interpreted within the early Palestinian church.[7] Concerning the self-consciousness of Jesus, Jeremias concludes that he certainly reckoned with the idea of his own violent death, that he must have thought about the meaning of that death, and that he drew upon Isaiah 53 to do so. Jeremias explains the relative scarcity of this connection in the early New Testament material through the hypothesis that Jesus spoke of this destiny only in private to his closest followers.[8]

Jeremias's argument that the portrait of the messiah in Judaism of this era included the concept of vicarious suffering to expiate the sins of Israel has found little support.[9] While the designation of the messiah as

3.   Zimmerli and Jeremias, *The Servant of God*, pp. 45-50.
4.   Zimmerli and Jeremias, *The Servant of God*, p. 53.
5.   Zimmerli and Jeremias, *The Servant of God*, pp. 54-78.
6.   Zimmerli and Jeremias, *The Servant of God*, p. 57.
7.   Zimmerli and Jeremias, *The Servant of God*, pp. 93-94.
8.   Zimmerli and Jeremias, *The Servant of God*, pp. 98-104.
9.   Among the more significant refutations are Morna Hooker, *Jesus and the Servant* (London: SPCK, 1959); and E. Lohse, *Märtyrer und Gottesknecht* (FRLANT, 64; Göttingen: Vandenhoeck & Ruprecht, 1966).

God's servant is found in a few places, these do not speak clearly of a *suffering* servant or messiah. The targum on Isaiah, for example, interprets all of 52.13–53.12 in reference to the messiah, but relocates suffering to Israel or to the enemies of the messiah. Most scholars would agree with the conclusion of J. Fitzmyer: 'The idea of a suffering messiah is found nowhere in the OT or in any Jewish literature prior to or contemporaneous with the NT.'[10] Rejecting the evidence cited by Jeremias as questionable or anachronistic, Fitzmyer concludes that '...it is highly questionable whether Isaian Servant passages...were ever interpreted in a messianic sense in pre-Christian Judaism'.[11] Only in later Jewish tradition was the Servant given the title of Messiah.[12]

If the connection between the Suffering Servant and the mission of the messiah is mostly missing in pre-Christian Judaism, it is not far to the conclusion that Jesus did not speak of himself in these terms. H. Conzelmann takes this position:

> In Judaism, 'servant' stands only at the periphery as a designation for the Messiah (IV Ezra: Syrian Baruch). But there is no thought of the suffering of the Messiah here, only of his glory.
>
> Jesus did not refer Isa. 53 to himself. This was only done by the community, because it found here the explanation of his death. It should be noted that where Isa. 53 is quoted, the title παῖς does not occur; where it occurs, there is no reference to suffering.[13]

O. Cullmann agrees on the background of the title, but reaches a different conclusion on its application.[14] He agrees that Judaism of the New Testament era did connect the name of the Servant to the messiah, but this was a messianism missing the idea of vicarious suffering and atoning death. Cullmann agrees that Jesus did not use the title, but he did apply the idea to himself. For Cullmann, Jesus saw himself as the fulfillment of both the suffering and the renewed covenant associated with the Servant of Deutero-Isaiah. The origin of this connection is to be found, says Cullmann, in the baptismal experience of Jesus. The voice which Jesus hears from heaven is citing Isa. 42.1. While *'ebed* has been translated with υἱός (son), Jesus heard here a call from God to fulfill the destiny of the Suffering Servant who restores God's covenant

10. Fitzmyer, *Luke*, p. 212.
11. Fitzmyer, *Luke*, p. 212.
12. Fitzmyer, *Luke*, p. 200.
13. Conzelmann, *An Outline*, p. 85.
14. Cullmann, *Christology*, pp. 51-82.

with Israel. This characterization of Jesus is preserved in the memory of the early Church, but it soon recedes because of early Church interest in the *present* work of Jesus as the risen Lord. For Cullmann, the Servant of God title and imagery are foundational:

> ...this Christological designation deserves more attention in contemporary theology than it usually receives, not only because it is one of the oldest answers to the question who Jesus is, but also because it goes back to Jesus himself and therefore opens to us most clearly the secret of his self-consciousness.[15]

The Servant title is used of Jesus in the New Testament only in Mt. 8.16-17; Acts 3.13, 26; 4.27, 30; and indirectly in Acts 8.26-40. Only Acts 3.13 and 4.27 connect suffering to the activity of Jesus as Servant. Beyond the New Testament the title appears in various liturgical settings (*Did.* 9.2-3; 10.2; *1 Clem.* 59), but here it is largely void of christological significance.

M. Karrer discusses one text from Qumran in which the Suffering Servant is linked in some ways to the messiah.[16] The text designated as 1QIsa changes the awkward *mischat* of Isa. 52.14b to *maschati*. This change alters the reading from 'his appearance was marred' to 'I have anointed him'. This interpretation thus connects the image of the Suffering Servant to the concept of God's anointed. Nonetheless, this tradition does not represent a distinct line of thought. There is no explicit reference to the messiah, only to an anointing. Furthermore, this variant reading remains isolated; it does not appear to have strong antecedants, nor does it generate a succession of texts with this reading of Isa. 52.14b. Karrer concludes that, in spite of 1QIsa, there is no widespread conception of the Servant of God who is honored for his suffering for others in the Judaism of the New Testament era.[17]

Thus, the Suffering Servant does not provide a clear messianic image or expectation in the Old Testament or in pre-Christian Judaism. As Fitzmyer notes,

> It is not surprising that the 'Servant' of Isaiah 52-53 was eventually identified with a messiah in the Jewish tradition; but it still remains to be shown that this identification existed in pre-Christian Judaism or in Judaism contemporary with the NT.[18]

15. Cullmann, *Christology*, p. 81.
16. Karrer, *Der Gesalbte*, pp. 364-65.
17. Karrer, *Der Gesalbte*, p. 365.
18. Fitzmyer, *Luke*, p. 1566.

Consequently the Servant imagery employed in the Gospel of Mark cannot be explained in terms of its background or in connection to the consciousness of Jesus. Whatever descriptive value the Servant imagery exercises within the Gospel of Mark must be evaluated as an acquired significance drawn from the structures and strategies of this Gospel.

The Literary Foreground

The Servant title (παῖς) is never used of Jesus in the Gospel of Mark. Nonetheless, a strong undercurrent of servant imagery flows through this narrative and contributes to its christological portrait.

This imagery focuses on the suffering of Jesus and is built almost exclusively upon allusions to the Old Testament. The concept of Jesus as the smitten shepherd (Mk 14.27) is drawn from Zech. 13.7: 'Strike the shepherd that the sheep may be scattered.' The Gethsemane lament in Mk 14.34—'My soul is troubled unto death'—is based on allusion to various Old Testament psalms.[19] The arrest of Jesus fulfills the Scriptures (14.49). The death scene (15.20c-37) portrays Jesus as the innocent sufferer from the Psalms.[20]

More significantly, the story of Jesus' death draws upon the Isaianic portrait of the Suffering Servant. Though the title is never employed, numerous elements from the Servant Songs (Isa 42.1-4; 49.1-6; 50.4-11; 52.13–54.12) influence the trial scenes.

Like the Servant, Jesus suffers and dies for 'the many' (Isa. 53.12; Mk 14.24). The silence of Jesus in the trial before the religious leaders (14.53-65) recalls Isa. 53.7: 'He was oppressed, and he was afflicted, yet he opened not his mouth...' This silence surfaces anew in the trial before Pilate (15.5). The amazement of Pilate (15.5) may signify the startling of the nations and the silencing of kings predicted in Isa. 52.15. The mockery scene of Mk 15.16-20 draws upon Old Testament images and shows their fulfillment in Jesus. He does not cry or lift up his voice (Isa. 42.2). He seems to have labored in vain and to have

19. See, e.g., Pss. 42.5, 6, 11; 43.5.

20. Rudolf Pesch, *Der Prozess Jesu geht weiter* (Freiburg: Herder, 1988), pp. 65-66, sees echoes of the following psalms: 22, 27, 31, 34, 35, 37, 38, ·39, 40, 41, 42, 43, 54, 55, 69, 71, 86, 88, 109, 118. See also Alfred Suhl, *Die Funktion der alttestamentlichen Zitate und Anspielungen im Markusevangelium* (Gütersloh: Gerd Mohn, 1965).

spent his strength for nothing (Isa. 49.4). Like the Servant of old, Jesus has given his back to the smiters, and he has not hid his face from shame and spitting (Isa. 50.6). In particular, the images of the fourth Servant Song (Isa 52.13–53.12) are fulfilled in Jesus:

a marred appearance	Isa. 52.14
despised and rejected	Isa. 53.3
a man of sorrows, acquainted with grief	Isa. 53.3-4
stricken, smitten, afflicted, wounded, bruised	Isa. 53.4-5
oppressed, afflicted	Isa. 53.7
silent in the face of judgment	Isa. 53.7
killed	Isa. 53.8, 9, 12

This link between service and suffering is not incidental. Jesus speaks of his own service on one occasion (Mk 10.45). Here the service of Jesus is given precise definition: he has come to give his life on behalf of the people. Like the Servant (Isa. 53.8, 12), the service of Jesus is his death for others (Mk 10.45). Thus, a reciprocal relation is established: the service of Jesus is manifested in his death, while the death of Jesus gathers unto him the Old Testament image of the Suffering Servant.

This subtle characterization developed within the heart of the story is confirmed, in retrospect, through the larger frame of the narrative. The initial scene of the Gospel characterizes Jesus as the Beloved Son in view of his baptism and his bearing of the Spirit (Mk 1.9-11). In a second reading, the reader may recognize here the opening lines of the first Servant Song:

> Behold my Servant, whom I uphold,
> my chosen, in whom my soul delights;
> I have put my Spirit upon him,
> he will bring forth justice to the nations (Isa. 42.1).

Thus, the reader who has learned to recognize the image of the Suffering Servant in the passion account may now find this identification in the opening lines of Jesus' story.[21]

Seen in this light, Mk 10.45 becomes a verbal hinge which takes up the initial characterization of Jesus as an obedient servant and connects

---

21. This identification of the Son and the Servant may be encouraged by passages which seem to employ *'ebed* in the sense of 'son'. See Deut. 32.43, various aspects of Wisdom literature such as Wis. 2.13, 18, Jn 4.46-54. This argument is supported by Bousset, *Kyrios Christos*; and by J. Jeremias, 'παῖς θεοῦ', *TDNT*, V, pp. 677-717. This position is debated by I.H. Marshall, *Jesus the Saviour: Studies in New Testament Theology* (London: SPCK, 1990), pp. 121-33.

it to the death of Jesus: he has come to serve, to give his life as a ransom on behalf of the many. In a similar manner the vineyard parable (Mk 12.1-12) takes up the identity of the Beloved Son (1.11) and extends its imagery from that of obedience to that of suffering and death: he is the Beloved Son who dies violently. This linguistic connection becomes a narrative reality in the story of Jesus' death, with its rich allusion to the Servant Songs.

Only in the closing verses of this Gospel is the suffering of Jesus given titular expression. Mark 16.6 refers to Jesus as τὸν ἐσταυρωμένον, the Crucified One, and confirms the fulfillment of the service proposed in Mk 10.45.

Thus, a type of narrative frame has been created around Jesus' destiny. The connection of Jesus to the Suffering Servant emanates from the passion story; neither the baptismal scene nor the saying in Mk 10.45 can evoke this image on its own strength. Once this connection is established through the events surrounding Jesus' death, the reader may trace this allusion behind the scene of Jesus' baptism. Subsequently, Mk 10.45 evokes this characterization and links it precisely to Jesus' death. The vineyard parable sustains similar connections. This service unto death becomes a titular acclamation in the closing verses of the narrative. Thus, the servant imagery may be seen, through retrospective reading, to frame the whole of Jesus' story. While the servant imagery belongs to the story of Jesus from beginning to end, the center and point of origin for this connection lies precisely in the passion account. The servant imagery is thus a passion metaphor which moves out from the scenes of Jesus' death to encompass the whole of his story. Despite the absence of the title, servant imagery provides a distinct pattern for characterization and for Christology in the Gospel of Mark.

Conclusion

The Servant of God title demonstrates the validity and necessity of analyzing titles as narrative constructions. Critical scholarship is not yet able to clarify the meaning of this title in pre-Christian Judaism. The place of the term in the consciousness of Jesus lies beyond scholarly reach. The early Church abandoned this title in favor of other descriptions. For diverse reasons the significance of the Servant of God imagery cannot be unveiled through its history of development.

Without dismissing these not-yet-answered questions, a formalist analysis of the servant imagery demonstrates its vital role in the christological portrait of this Gospel. The narrative makes no claim that Jesus spoke of himself in this manner, and no proof texts cite Jesus as the fulfillment of these prophecies. Nonetheless, the narrative employs various strategies and patterns to connect the servant imagery to Jesus. Despite the ambiguity of its historical content, the servant image is endowed by the scheme of this Gospel with persuasive descriptive power. It is Jesus' story which provides the standards by which to interpret this title, and not the reverse. In the faithful suffering of Jesus the mission of the Servant is defined and realized.

Chapter 11

SON OF DAVID

> And when he heard that it is Jesus the Nazarene, he began to cry out and to say, 'Son of David, have mercy on me' (Mk 10.47).

The Son of David provides one of the few terms with a clear line of messianic development within the Old Testament and Judaism. Seen over against this heritage, the role of this title in the Gospel of Mark proves distinctive.

The Historical Background

Within the Old Testament there developed a clear expectation of the continuation of the Davidic rule over Israel. Historical realities transformed this into a hope for the renewal of the Davidic rule. In the Judaism of the first century BCE this hope took on clear messianic lines.

The promise of 2 Sam. 7.12-16 provided the basis of this hope:

> When your days are fulfilled and you lie down with your ancestors, I will raise up your offspring after you, who shall come forth from your body, and I will establish his kingdom. He shall build a house for my name, and I will establish the throne of his kingdom forever. I will be a father to him, and he shall be a son to me. When he commits iniquity, I will punish him with a rod such as mortals use, with blows inflicted by human beings. But I will not take my steadfast love from him, as I took it from Saul, whom I put away from before you. Your house and your kingdom shall be made sure forever before me; your throne shall be established forever. In accordance with all these words and with all this vision, Nathan spoke to David.

While political events destroyed the hope of a continuous Davidic kingship, the hope of a restored Davidic monarchy endured. This hope was at times connected to the images of the Balaam prophecy in Num. 24.17:

I see him, but not now; I behold him, but not near—
a star shall come out of Jacob, and a scepter shall rise out of Israel;
it shall crush the borderlands of Moab, and the territory of all the Shethites.

Various terms were used to express the relationship of this hope to King David. He is known in Isa. 11.10 as the 'Sprout of Jesse' and elsewhere as the 'Shoot (of David)' (Jer. 23.5; 33.15; Zech. 3.8; 6.12). Other instances refer to this figure as 'David' in a metaphorical sense, since the historical David is dead (Ezek. 34.23-24). The emphasis is not simply on the personal reign of this figure, but on the kingdom which he represents: 'On that day I will raise up the booth of David that is fallen, and repair its breaches, and raise up its ruins, and rebuild it as in the days of old' (Amos 9.11). Thus, the idea that God will raise up a future leader in the pattern of David to restore and lead Israel is widespread in the thought of the Old Testament.

The title Son of David is first attached to this hope in the first century BCE. This seems to happen in response to the fall of the Hasmonean dynasty and the loss of Israel's political independence to the Romans. The Pharisaic expression of this hope is articulated in *Psalms of Solomon* 17. The promise of an unending Davidic kingdom is recalled: 'Lord, you chose David to be king over Israel, and swore to him about his descendants forever, that his kingdom should not fail before you' (*Pss. Sol.* 17.4). The intrusion of other forces has broken the Davidic line (*Pss. Sol.* 17.5-20). The prayer for the restoration of the Davidic rule stands at the center of this text, and the leader is described as Son of David: 'See, Lord, and raise up for them their king, the Son of David, to rule over your servant Israel in the time known to you, O God' (*Pss. Sol.* 17.21). The activity of this leader takes two directions: he will conquer all who oppress Israel (*Pss. Sol.* 17.22-25), and he will re-establish Jerusalem and Israel as the righteous people of God (*Pss. Sol.* 17.26-32). This Davidic king is called the 'Lord Messiah' (χριστός κύριος).[1]

The Son of David expectation emerges at other points in pre-Christian Judaism. Qumran writings look forward to the 'Shoot of David who will come with the investigator of the Law in...Zi[on at the en]d of the days...' (4QFlor 1.11-13; see also 4QpIsa Fr.D1). Various

---

1. While many scholars see here a Christian emendation, this is not necessary. The Greek and Syriac manuscripts are uniform in reading 'Lord Messiah', and there is no textual evidence for reading 'Lord's Messiah'. See the argument by R.B. Wright in 'Psalms of Solomon', *OTP*, II, pp. 639-70 (667-68) n. 'z'.

Qumran texts build upon the Balaam prophecy of Num. 24.17, as does the *Testament of the Twelve Patriarchs* (see the Armenian version of *T. Jud.* 24).[2]

This expection plays a significant role in the New Testament and in early Christianity. A primitive two-stage Christology points to the messianic quality of Jesus' earthly activity as the Son of David. According to Rom. 1.3-4, Jesus is 'from the seed of David according to the flesh'. A more lofty status is described in the second stage of this Christology: Jesus is 'marked off as Son of God in power according to the spirit of holiness by resurrection from the dead' (Rom. 1.4). The final acclamation of this early Christology is 'Jesus Christ our Lord' (Rom. 1.4). This two-stage Christology is also seen in 2 Tim. 2.8. Jesus Christ, who has been raised from the dead, is remembered as one who descended from David. Thus, the Davidic sonship of Jesus describes his messianic status as an earthly figure, but this status is followed by his elevation to a loftier status. This two-stage Christology may also underlie the discussion of Mk 12.35-37 and its parallels. The question addressed there is how one who is designated Son of David can also be designated his Lord, as in Ps. 110.1.

The Son of David title is absent in the Sayings Tradition, and it is infrequent in the Gospels. As in the primitive tradition, the Gospels use Son of David images to refer to Jesus' earthly life. Luke's infancy stories emphasize Jesus' origin from the house of David (Lk. 1.32, 69; 3.31). Matthew gives even stronger focus to this Davidic origin (Mt. 1.1). Matthew then introduces the Son of David title in stories from Jesus' life (Mt. 9.27; 12.23; 15.22; 21.9, 15). The Fourth Gospel reports a division over the origin of the Messiah in light of Davidic expectations (Jn 7.41).

These earthly attributes are transformed in the Revelation. Here Jesus is called the 'Root of David' (ἡ ῥίζα Δαυίδ in Rev. 5.5; 22.16). Drawing upon Isa. 11.1, 10 and 22.22, this tradition highlights the eschatological role of Jesus in the salvation of God. Jesus holds the key of David (Rev. 3.7), and he is the descendant of David (22.16). In this way an earthly messianic term is transferred to the glorified Christ.

The Son of David Christology endured into early Christianity. In this tradition the Davidic descent of Jesus is emphasized as a prelude and contrast to his status as Son of God (Ignatius, *Eph.* 20.2; *Smyrn.* 1.1;

---

2. This possibility is discussed by Burger, *Jesus als Davidssohn*, pp. 21-22.

Trall. 9; *Eph.* 18.2). *4 Ezra* relates a vision of a lion and explains that 'this is the Messiah whom the Most High has kept until the end of days, who will arise from the offspring of David...' (*4 Ezra* 12.32). This tradition combines Jewish and Christian influence and emerges around 100 CE.

The expectation of a messiah who is Son of David endures into rabbinical Judaism. The Messiah was understood to come from Davidic descent, and he was sometimes addressed as David. This hope focused more on the messianic age brought by this figure than on the personality of the Messiah.[3] The hope for a messianic Son of David is sustained in the worship practices of the synagogue. In the Palestinian rescension, the fourteenth Benediction asks God's mercy 'on the kingdom of the house of David, of the Messiah of thy righteousness'. The fifteenth Benediction of the Babylonian rescension says 'May the shoot of David sprout forth quickly, and may his horn be lifted up by thy help. Blessed be Thou, Yahweh, who dost cause the horn of help to shoot forth'. A similar request is found in the Habhinenu Prayer and in the Musaph Prayer.[4]

This evidence shows that a long line of expectation arose within the Old Testament and developed within Judaism and within early Christianity. With the exception of the apocalyptic transformations of the Revelation, this tradition speaks throughout of an earthly deliverer who will in some way fulfill the hopes of Israel. This figure is nowhere outside of Christianity designated with the title Son of God.[5] This expectation points to a human Messiah who delivers Israel through his earthly activity. He is 'a thoroughly human figure. He is above all ruler and king; and indeed he is entirely and alone for the people of Israel.'[6]

Thus, a clear messianic expectation developed around the Son of David title. Though various types of messianic activity are expected under this title, a wide stream of Old Testament and Jewish tradition awaits an earthly descendant of David who will restore Israel.

3. See E. Lohse, 'υἱὸς Δαυίδ', *TDNT*, VIII, pp. 481-82.

4. Lohse, 'υἱὸς Δαυίδ', pp. 481-82.

5. So Burger, *Jesus als Davidssohn*, p. 23; but see the description in 2 Sam. 7.14; Ps. 2.7; Ps. 89.

6. W. Bousset and H. Gressmann, *Die Religion des Judentums im spät-hellenistischen Zeitalter* (HNT, 21; Tübingen: J.C.B. Mohr, 3rd edn, 1926).

The Literary Foreground

Son of David provides one of the few christological titles with a coherent historical development and clear messianic implications. Over against this historical background the Gospel of Mark constructs its own patterns around the Son of David title.

Distribution

The Son of David title occurs in two scenes within a narrow span of the Gospel of Mark (10.47, 48; 12.35, 37). In Mk 10.46-53 Jesus is twice addressed as υἱὲ Δαυίδ by Bartimaeus. The scene in 12.35-37 belongs to the larger cycle of Jesus' teaching in the Temple (12.35). Following a series of inquiries (11.13-17, 18-27, 28-34) in which he silences his challengers (12.34), Jesus poses a question of his own (12.35-37). This question presents a christological riddle: how can the Messiah be David's son if David calls him Lord? Within this christological discussion the υἱὸς Δαυίδ imagery is employed twice (12.35, 37).

Association

Two images are gathered around the Son of David title. Bartimaeus's cry in Mk 10.47, 48 carries an insistent expectation of mercy and healing. The riddle in 12.35-37 suggests the Messiah will be lord over Davidic tradition. Significantly, both scenes are connected to Jerusalem, the city of David. The plea in 10.47, 48 provides the final stage of Jesus' journey to Jerusalem. At the close of the scene Bartimaeus follows Jesus 'in the way' (10.52)—a path which leads immediately to Jerusalem (11.1). The christological riddle of 12.35-37 is set within the confines of Jerusalem. More significantly, the question is posed from the Temple (12.35) which David first conceived. From this standpoint the significance of the riddle becomes clear: the Christ is lord over all of Davidic tradition, including the Temple.[7] The narrative thus produces two associations around the Son of David title: (1) the powerful mercy of Jesus, and (2) the authority of the Messiah over Davidic tradition, including Jerusalem and the Temple.

---

7.   See also Mk 14.58, where Jesus' opposition to the Temple is brought as a charge against him. This conflict is a widespread image in the Gospel of Mark.

Confirmation
The narrative does nothing to confirm or deny the υἱὸς Δαυίδ title. Jesus responds to the plea of Bartimaeus (10.49, 51-52), but makes no reference to the Son of David title. The healing act is associated with Jesus himself, with no direct connection to the title (10.52). Conversely, the scene in 12.35-37 is abstracted from the person of Jesus. The riddle involves the role of the Messiah over Davidic tradition, and no direct tie is made to the work of Jesus. While the narrative makes this connection abundantly clear at other points (1.1; 14.61-62), the debate in 12.35-37 remains abstract.

Development
No further developments are made upon the Son of David title. Jesus is linked to Nazareth (1.9, 24; 10.47; 14.67; 16.7) rather than the Davidic village of Bethlehem. Jerusalem, the city of David's glory, is the place of Jesus' demise. The Temple conceived by David is cleansed with prophetic zeal (11.15-19). The religious practices of Israel are condemned (12.1-12), and the destruction of the city and its Temple is foretold (13.2, 3-37). The image of Jesus as King is abandoned.[8] In the Gospel of Mark, Son of David remains an ambivalent and uncertain description of Jesus.

Effect
As a consequence of these formal patterns the Son of David imagery stands over against its historical background. The Son of David title is employed in two isolated scenes in close proximity to Jerusalem. Associated with the title are images of the powerful mercy of Jesus and the authority of the Messiah over all Davidic tradition. The narrative neither confirms nor negates the title, and no further development occurs. Consequently, the Son of David title remains a largely isolated and undefined image in the Gospel of Mark.

Conclusion

The Son of David title illustrates the danger of reading the history of a tradition into the world of a narrative. Within the Gospel of Mark Jesus is not the Davidic conquerer of earlier expectation. There is no dogmatic separation between his earthly work and heavenly status as found

---

8. See Chapter 6 on the title of King.

in later Christian thought. Formalistic analysis shows that the Gospel of Mark withdraws from the traditional lines of development without negating the Son of David title. In the environs of Jerusalem Jesus is addressed as Son of David, but his response is characterized by healing and mercy. Standing within the city of David Jesus asserts the priority of the Messiah over Davidic tradition, including the Temple. Through this pattern of placement and connection the Son of David image plays a minor part in a complex characterization of Jesus.

Through this process a decisive hermeneutical transition may be observed. Titles should no longer be seen as pre-fabricated descriptions applied to the life of Jesus. Indeed, a process of definition and redefinition may be seen at work in these narratives. The impact of the Jesus event and the strategies of the narratives which relate that event exert a creative influence upon traditional images. Titles can no longer be seen as ready-made definitions which clarify the Jesus event and the stories of Jesus; they may serve instead as reflections which are shaped by the realities of Jesus. To some degree, Jesus has become the *hermeneusis* of all messianic titles and messianic conceptions. Thus, the Son of David has been redefined in the story of Jesus.

Chapter 12

SON OF GOD

And the unclean spirits, whenever they were seeing him, were falling
before him and were crying out, 'You are the Son of God' (Mk 3.11).

The Son of God title has an extensive, diverse background in the history of religions. It played a role in the thought of Egypt, in Hellenism,
and in the Roman world. The term is also important in the thought
world of the Old Testament and within Judaism. The christological use
of Son of God stands within this wide-ranging tradition.

The Historical Background

The Son of God title was used in the ancient Near East as a designation
of rulers. This was especially true in Egypt, where the pharaohs were
regarded as children of the sun god Re and were called 'sons of God'.
This sonship was generally established through a rite of enthronement,
and some have argued that this pattern influenced Hebrew thought at
points (Ps. 2.2, 7). In this sense Oriental kings were considered physical
children of the divinity.[1] Within the Hellenistic and Roman world
the Son of God title was applied to a variety of individuals. Rulers,
mythical heroes, wonder workers, and famous historical figures were
described by this title. The sense of this designation is clear and
consistent: 'In such a context the use of this title implied divine favor,
divine adoption, and even divine power, being conferred often at the
time of enthronement.'[2]

---

1.   See C.J. Gadd, *Ideas of Divine Rule in the Ancient East* (London: Oxford
University Press, 1948), pp. 45-50; H. Frankfort, *Kingship and the Gods* (Chicago:
University of Chicago Press, 1948), pp. 299-301. These ideas are discussed by
Fitzmyer, *Luke*, pp. 205-206. See also the discussion by W. von Martitz, 'υἱός',
TDNT, VIII, pp. 336-40.
2.   Fitzmyer, *Luke*, p. 206.

Working within the history of religions school of interpretation, Rudolf Bultmann saw this conception of the Son of God behind most of the New Testament use of this title. Bultmann believed that Rom. 1.3 and the transfiguration story of Mk 9.7 go back to an early Christian tradition which called Jesus the Son of God because of his resurrection. He saw the other instances in a different light: '...the synoptic passages in which Jesus is called Son of God are mostly either secondary and of Hellenistic-Christian origin, or else were formulated by the respective evangelist...'[3]

Most scholars trace a more direct Hebraic influence upon the New Testament use of Son of God. Within the world of the Old Testament various angelic figures and members of the council of Yahweh were seen as God's sons (Gen. 6.2, 4; Job 1.6; 2.1; 38.7; Dan. 3.25; Pss. 29.1; 89.6; 82.6; Deut. 32.8). These terms may represent a pattern of transition in which ideas from Canaanite religion are brought under the framework of Hebraic monotheism.

Three Old Testament references speak of the king as God's son (2 Sam 7.14; Pss. 2.7; 89.26-37). The prophecy of Nathan in 2 Sam. 7.8-17 tells of the promise to David that one of his descendants will be established by God over an unending kingdom. This human figure will be chastized by God for sin, but he will not be abandoned: 'Your house and your kingdom shall be made sure forever before me; your throne shall be established forever' (2 Sam. 7.16). The Davidic descendant who fulfills this promise is called God's son: 'I will be a father to him, and he shall be a son to me' (2 Sam. 7.14).

A similar image is found in Ps. 2.7. God has set a king upon Zion, the holy hill (2.6). Here the Lord rules through the anointed one (2.2). The warfare of the nations is against both the Lord and the Lord's anointed (2.2). Yahweh will fight on behalf of this king and will give him the nations as his heritage (2.8). This anointed king over Israel is called God's son: 'I will tell of the decree of the Lord: He said to me, "You are my son; today I have begotten you"' (2.7). Thus, the Son of God image applies here to a present, historical figure who has been anointed by God as king over Israel.

The idea of the king of Israel as the anointed one who is God's son is also present in Psalm 89. The steadfast love of God is recalled in the covenant made with David, the chosen one (89.3-4, 29, 36-37). The psalmist is reminded in a vision that David is the anointed one of God,

3. Bultmann, *Theology of the New Testament*, I, p. 50.

and that God will crush his enemies (89.20-25). The anointed king is the Son of God: 'He shall cry to me, "You are my Father, my God, and the Rock of my salvation!" I will make him the firstborn, the highest of the kings of the earth' (89.26-27).

Thus, the Old Testament understands kingship within Israel in terms of God's anointing. David and his descendants provide the primary models for this image. Through David and his line Yahweh will rule over Israel and against the nations which oppress it. The rule of God over Israel is established through God's intitiative: God will choose and anoint Davidic kings over Israel without end. They will be God's sons.

More frequent in the Old Testament is the reference to Israel as God's son. Israel is the firstborn of Yahweh (Exod. 4.22; Jer. 31.9) and God's dear child (Jer. 31.20). This heritage is rooted in God's election of Israel: 'When Israel was a child, I loved him, and out of Egypt I called my son' (Hos. 11.1). The people of Israel are the sons and daughters of God (Deut. 14.1; 32.5, 19; Isa. 43.6; 45.11; Hos. 2.1). Both Israel as a whole and individuals within Israel are God's children (Deut. 32.5-6, 18-19). While this imagery may echo the physical descent prevalent in ancient Near East religious thought, the Hebraic concept comes to mean that Yahweh has chosen and installed Israel as God's son.

These Old Testament patterns endured within pre-Christian Judaism. In the Septuagint the term for Beloved Son is taken from the Isaac narrative (Gen. 22.2, 12, 16) and applied to Ephraim (Jer. 38.20). The designation of Israel as God's son(s) continues through this period (Deut. 32.43 LXX; Exod. 4.22; Wis. 2.16, 18; 9.7; 18.4, 13; *Pss. Sol.* 17.27; Jdt. 9.4; Greek Est. 8.12q; Ecclus 36.16; *3 Macc.* 6.28).

The term is applied with great hesitancy to individuals during this period. The promised Davidic king is seen as God's son in agreement with the Hebrew texts of these promises. Apart from citation of these passages, the Son of God is rare in connection with individual figures. The upright Jew is called a son of God in Ecclus 4.10 and in Wis. 2.18.

There may be some connection between the messiah and the Son of God title in the Qumran literature. 4QFlor 1-2.1.10 names the 'Shoot of David' as God's son in its quotation of 2 Sam. 7.14.[4] J. Fitzmyer has identified an Aramaic text from Qumran which speaks of the 'Son of

---

4.   Fitzmyer, *Luke*, pp. 206-207, discusses this text.

God' and the 'Son of the Most High', though these terms may be non-messianic in this context.[5]

Thus, it is difficult to demonstrate a clear messianic expectation around the Son of God title in the Old Testament or in pre-Christian Judaism. While the term is connected to the future Davidic king who, like other kings, will be anointed and installed by God, reference to a distinct individual as the messianic Son of God is difficult to establish.[6]

Over against this clouded line of development the New Testament insists that Jesus the Messiah is the Son of God. Various concepts are emphasized by the New Testament use of this title. A primitive Christology contrasted the earthly work of Jesus as Son of David with his post-resurrection status as Son of God (Rom. 1.4). This conception is affirmed in Acts 13.33, where the resurrection marks the beginning of Jesus' sonship. This pronouncement occurs at the baptism of Jesus in the synoptics (Mk 1.11 and parallels). This experience is confirmed in the transfiguration story (Mk 9.7 and parallels). Other traditions establish the sonship of Jesus from his birth (Lk. 1.32-33, 35; Mt. 2.14-15). Eventually formulas of faith focus on the sending of the Son by God

5.   J. Fitzmyer, 'The Contribution of Qumran Aramaic to the Study of the New Testament' *NTS* 20 (1973–74), pp. 382-407.

6.   So Fitzmyer, *Luke*, p. 206: '...the full title is never found in the OT predicated directly of a future, expected Messiah'; Lohse, 'υἱός', p. 361: 'Thus far there is no clear instance to support the view that in pre-Christian times Judaism used the title "son of God" for the Messiah'; E. Schweizer, 'υἱός', *TDNT*, VIII, pp. 354-57 (355-56), detects less reticence in Hellenistic Judaism than in Palestinian Judaism; Cullmann, *Christology*, p. 279: 'It seems to me that the decisive consideration is that on the basis of the Old Testament and later Jewish views there is no apparent ground whatever for the early Church to designate Jesus as the Son of God. Even if theoretically we must reckon with the possibility that in connection with the conception of the king, the Jewish Messiah was now and then called "Son of God", the complete lack of proof for his being given such a title indicates at least that it was not an essential attribute of the Messiah'; Conzelmann, *An Outline*, p. 76: '...there is no evidence in Judaism for the use of the title "Son of God" for the Messiah.' Bultmann, Cullmann, and Riesenfeld keep open the possibility that Judaism, outside of the extant literature, spoke of the messiah as Son of God. Hahn, *Titles*, p. 284, believes this connection must have been present in pre-Christian Judaism: 'It emerges that the motif of the divine sonship in its distinctive form, therefore in the sense of appointment to office and assignment of dominion, practically belongs to royal messianism within the sphere of Palestinian late Judaism. It is extremely probable that there also the titular use of "Son of the Blessed" and the like had come to be common already in pre-Christian tradition.'

(Gal. 4.4-5; Rom. 8.3-4; Jn 3.16-21). The New Testament develops various aspects of this sonship in its descriptions of Jesus.

The Literary Foreground

The portrait of Jesus as the Son of God in the Gospel of Mark stands at a delicate juncture between the generalized images of the Old Testament and Judaism and the confessional certainty of early Christianity. The sonship of Jesus is not primarily an inherited or an assumed image in the Gospel of Mark; it is an image constructed and defined with care through the developments of the narrative.

Distribution

The Son of God description (υἱοῦ θεοῦ) occurs eight times in the Gospel of Mark. The Son of God title is found in 1.1; 3.11; 5.7; 15.39.[7] Jesus is refered to as the Beloved Son (ὁ υἱός μου ὁ ἀγαπητός) in 1.11 and 9.7.[8] The Son of the Blessed One (ὁ υἱός τοῦ εὐλογητοῦ) is found in 14.61. The absolute use of the title (ὁ υἱός) is found in 13.32. These various expressions are evenly distributed across the narrative and are employed by various actants. In the superscript the narrator clarifies the identity of Jesus as Messiah and Son of God (1.1). The divine voice declares the sonship of Jesus at his baptism (1.11). Demons acknowledge the sonship of Jesus in 3.11 and in 5.7. The divine acclamation is repeated in 9.7. Jesus himself refers to the Son in 13.32. The sonship title is part of the central question at the trial before the religious authorities, and Jesus affirms the title in 14.62. The centurion's confession provides the final occurance and the only use of the title by a human other than Jesus in the Gospel of Mark (15.39).

Association

A few vital associations are created around the Son title. Sonship is linked to the Christ title in 1.1 and in 14.61. The title is connected to Jesus' authority over demons in 3.11 and 5.7. The divine voice of 1.11 acclaims Jesus as one in whom 'I am well pleased' (εὐδόκησα). The acclamation in 9.7 points to the authority of Jesus' teaching and is

7. Some manuscripts (ℵ* θ (28) *pc*; Or) omit υἱοῦ θεοῦ from Mk 1.1; the stronger evidence favors inclusion (ℵ' BDLW *pc* [*sed* του θ. A f[1.13] 𝔐] latt sy co; Ir[lat]).

8. The reference to a beloved son in Mk 12.6 may be seen as a metaphorical reference to Jesus.

sandwiched between two passion teachings (8.27–9.1; 9.11-13, 30-32). Mark 13.32 declares the limits on the Son's knowledge of the last days. Mark 14.61-62 links the Son to the coming power of the Son of Man. The centurion's confession in 15.39 creates the strongest narrative association. This confession is linked explicitly to the death of Jesus: 'But the centurion, standing before him, beholding that he died in this manner, said, "Truly this man was Son of God".'

The narrative thus employs a few loose associations to clarify the Son title. Jesus' sonship is associated with his authority over demons (3.11; 5.7) and with the authority of his instruction (9.7). The power of the coming Son of Man is connected to Jesus' sonship (14.61-62). Alongside this authority, the submission of the Son is focused. The Son is pleasing to God (1.11), and he knows less than the Father (9.7). The teaching of the Son focuses on his suffering (8.27–9.1; 9.2-10, 11-13, 30-32), and the Son is first confessed by another human being in view of his death (15.39). Consequently the narrative associates sonship terminology with two contrasting images: authority and submissive suffering.

Confirmation
The Gospel of Mark wholly confirms the validity of the Son title. Several techniques establish this positive role for the term. (1) The narrator informs the reader from the beginning (1.1). (2) The sonship of Jesus is affirmed on two occasions by an external witness with divine authority (1.11; 9.7). (3) Supernatural forces also acclaim the sonship of Jesus (3.11; 5.7). (4) The dramatic reply of Jesus in 14.62 (ἐγώ εἰμι) confirms his identity as the Son of God. (5) The negative use of the title is found only with Jesus' opponents (14.61-64). Only the absolute reference of 13.32 remains ambiguous. As a consequence the narrative supports and affirms the Son title as a valid description of Jesus.

Development
The Gospel of Mark develops this title into a central christological image. The narrative employs two techniques to generate this portrait. First, the various elements associated with the Son title create contrasting images. Jesus' sonship is marked by authority (3.11; 5.7; 9.7; 14.61-62), but also by submission, limitation and suffering (1.11; 9.7; 13.32; 15.39). These contrasting themes blend into an unexpected narrative claim: Jesus expresses the authority of his sonship precisely through submission, obedience, suffering and death.

Secondly, a primary pattern of development is found in the framing technique employed in connection with this title. The Son title serves as a bold assertion of Jesus' identity, but with little direct explication. As with the Christ title, this rather bare use of the Son title may be explained in one of three ways: (1) by the assumption of a common understanding of the title based on shared historical or sociological perspectives; (2) by an inappropriate or incompetent use of the term; (3) by a narrative strategy which defines the title not from historical or etymological preconceptions, but through the structures and moves of the narrative. The Gospel of Mark employs the third technique. The narrative creates a limited number of associations, but it employs the term to create the structural and ideological frame of the narrative.

The acclamation of Jesus' sonship echoes throughout the narrative (1.1, 11; 3.11; 5.7; 9.7; 14.61-62; 15.39). The acclamation is validated not only by this narrative echo, but also by the authority of those who acknowledge Jesus as the Son: the narrator, supernatural beings, the Christ, the divine voice. The most important of these claims stand at the beginning and the end of the narrative. The opening lines of the text proclaim Jesus' sonship without apology or explication (1.1). This narrative claim is given divine sanction at the beginning of the story line (1.11). The climactic confession of Jesus' sonship is found in 14.61-62 (not in 15.39). The question of Jesus' sonship provides the basis of his trial and condemnation: 'Are you the Christ, the Son of the Blessed One?' asks the chief priest (14.61). The answer of Jesus is an unambiguous reply which invokes the power and name of Yahweh: 'ἐγώ εἰμι [I am]' (14.62). This passage provides Jesus' singular confession of his sonship and the climactic acclamation of the narrative. The confession of 15.39 marks the first entrance of this established truth into the realm of human response.

The narrative thus frames the entire story with the divinely sanctioned claim that Jesus is Son of God (1.1; 14.62). This claim is echoed through the stages of the narrative and confirmed by voices of authority. However, the Son of God title invades the level of human response only gradually and with limited success. The impact of this title owes as much to the frame of the story as to the substance of the story.

Effect
Through strategic use of the υἱός title the whole story of Jesus is placed under the hermeneutic of his identity as the Son of God. The primary

development of the Son of God title is not through the images associated directly with the title, but through the strategic gathering of all the elements of the story under the governance of the Son of God title. Various images and assertions not directly associated with the title may now be taken up as aspects of Jesus' sonship. Not just selected elements of the story, but the whole of the story becomes explication, demonstration, and commentary on Jesus' sonship. The story expends little energy in direct defense or explication of the Son title since the story itself serves as commentary on the identity of the Son. As a result, various unattached details of the story line—wonders, controversies, teaching, other titles—become statements of Christology which operate under and explicate the titular claims of Mk 1.1 and 14.62. The narrative frame insists, with divine sanction, *that* Jesus is Son of God; the stories set within that frame tell *how* Jesus is Son of God. Through this strategy the narrative constructs the Son title as a complex, deeply-nuanced christological image.

Conclusion

The image of Jesus as Son of God stands in the Gospel of Mark at a delicate juncture in the development of this tradition. The Gospel of Mark is more certain and more coherent in its messianic claim than most of its Hebraic and Jewish predecessors and parallels. At the same time the Gospel of Mark is less dogmatic and more demonstrative than most of early Christianity in its presentation of Jesus as Son of God. On the one hand Son of God is designated as a definitive title and is attached without apology to the historical figure of Jesus. On the other hand this Gospel offers its entire story as definition and demonstration of its claim that Jesus is Son of God.

The primary shaping of this image lies not in the prehistory or the preconception of the term, but in the artistic manipulation of the Son of God title within the world of this Gospel. Ultimately this sonship imagery gains its primary christological value within a literary context: the sonship title presents a narrative portrait and a narrative demand. Like all of the titles, Son of God belongs first and foremost to a setting of proclamation, call, and claim. It belongs to the kerygma, the Gospel story of Jesus, who is Messiah and Son of God.

Chapter 13

SON OF MAN

'And you shall see the Son of Man seated at the right hand of power and coming with the clouds of heaven' (Mk 14.62).

The Son of Man title emerges from a diverse cluster of images drawn from the Old Testament, from Jewish apocalyptic thought, and from non-Jewish traditions. Even the linguistic basis of this term proves elusive. The use of the term in the New Testament and early Christianity is equally perplexing. Despite this ambiguity, the importance of the Son of Man title cannot be avoided, particularly within the narrative world of the Gospel of Mark.

The Historical Background

Scholars disagree on the role of the Aramaic description which underlies the Son of Man title.[1] Behind the Greek phrase (ὁ υἱός τοῦ ἀνθρώπου) stands the Hebrew *ben 'adam* and the Aramaic *bar 'enas*. This Semitic expression employs a noun for humanity in general, but it individualizes that noun through its construction. The term thus refers to 'one who belongs to the human classification'.[2] The phrase could also be used indefinitely to mean 'someone'. This use of the term

1. On the linguistic aspects of this title and other issues of the current debate, see Vermes, *Jesus the Jew*; idem, 'The "Son of Man" Debate', *JSNT* 1 (1978), pp. 19-32; J. Fitzmyer, *A Wandering Aramean: Collected Aramaic Essays* (Missoula, MT: Scholars Press, 1979), pp. 143-60; idem, 'Another View of the "Son of Man" Debate', *JSNT* 4 (1979), pp. 58-68; Lindars, *Jesus Son of Man*; W. Walker, 'The Son of Man: Some Recent Developments', *CBQ* 45 (1983), pp. 584-607; John R. Donahue, 'Recent Studies on the Origin of "Son of Man" in the Gospel', *CBQ* 48 (1986), pp. 484-98.

2. Cullmann, *Christology*, p. 138. The German *Menschenkind* is composed of the term for 'human beings' and the term for 'child'. This combination results in the meaning of 'a human person'.

surfaces in the Old Testament, particularly within poetic parallelism.[3] In each expression the phrase appears in the second part of synonymous parallelism as emphatic repetition of a term designating a human being.[4] The Hebrew form of this concept (but not the Aramaic) may be used as a direct address. The Hebrew expression *ben 'adam* is used over 90 times in Ezekial. In Ezekial the term is used by God to address the prophet, but its meaning is unclear. The term most likely refers to the prophet as a human, in contrast to Yahweh. Others see *bar 'enas* as a circumlocution for the speaker.[5] Thus, the linguistic evidence points to four uses for this term: (1) As a generic term it would mean 'a human being'; (2) As an indefinite term it would mean 'someone'; (3) As a circumlocution for the speaker it would mean 'I'; (4) As direct address it could point to a human figure or to one who is more than human. The key issue raised by this linguistic data is how a term with generic, indefinite, or deflected reference to one human can take on the technical theological status found in later writings.

C. Colpe suggests a backdrop for the apocalyptic Son of Man imagery in Canaanite mythology.[6] The story of a young god taking the power of an old god circulated in Canaanite mythology and may be seen in the rivalry between Baal and El in the Ras Shamra texts. The transfer of dominion from the Ancient of Days to the Son of Man, as seen in Daniel 7, may reflect this pattern. Colpe is careful to note that this tradition has no direct impact on Jewish apocalyptic thought or that of the New Testament; it may, however, provide the conceptual material from which later traditions developed.

A few scholars find connections in the Adam speculation found in rabbinical thought, in Philo, and in the *Pseudo-Clementines*.[7] While this concept originates in speculation about the Original Man who stands at the beginning of time, it develops both heavenly and eschatological aspects. Most scholars question the impact of this conceptual line upon the synoptics.

3. George Nickelsburg discusses this use in 'Son of Man', *ABD*, VI, p. 137.

4. See Num. 23.19; Isa. 51.12; 56.2; Jer. 49.18, 33; 50.40; 51.43; Ps. 8.4; 80.17; 146.3; Job 16.21; 25.6; 35.8.

5. Vermes supports this position, but Fitzmyer opposes it for the New Testament era.

6. C. Colpe, 'ὁ υἱός τοῦ ἀνθρώπου', *TDNT*, VIII, pp. 400-77, especially pp. 415-20.

7. Cullmann, *Christology*, pp. 142-52 sees this line as an important background for the New Testament usage.

A more likely connection is to be found in the thought world of Jewish apocalypticism. This tradition first emerges around 165 BCE in the book of Daniel. Further developments may be seen in the *Similitudes of Enoch* (*1 En.* 37–71). Traces of this tradition, without the title, are perhaps found in the Wisdom of Solomon, in *4 Ezra* and in *2 Baruch*. Only the Daniel passage can be certified as pre-Christian.

Daniel 7 presents a stark apocalyptic vision which employs Son of Man language. Daniel is given access to occurances in the heavenly court. Here he sees four beasts (Dan. 7.2-7). The fourth beast sprouts its eleventh horn, which has human eyes and speaks arrogant words (7.8). Within this context the Ancient of Days is described, and the scene of judgment begins (7.9-10). In the scene which follows the fourth beast is destroyed and the power of the others removed (7.11-12). Apparently in a separate scene, the Ancient One hands over dominion to a figure who comes with the clouds of heaven (7.13-14). This figure is described as 'one like a son of man'. While this phrase has been variously interpreted, it seems to refer to a heavenly figure who, in contrast to the beasts, bears human visage.[8] This figure represents the suffering people of God, and they share in his dominion (7.27).[9] The figure who appears before the Ancient One thus seems to be 'the enthroned heavenly patron of the people of God who have suffered at the hands of the kings, who have rebelled against heaven...'[10] In this instance the heavenly figure is *like* a son of man (in contrast to the beasts). Later texts will describe such a figure as the Son of Man.[11]

The apocalyptic image of a heavenly Son of Man emerges in clear fashion in the *Similitudes of Enoch* (*1 En.* 37–71). While the discoveries at Qumran demonstrate the pre-Christian existence of *1 Enoch*, the *Similitudes* are not found among this material. Consequently most scholars hesitate to date the *Similitudes* as pre-Christian. The modification of the Daniel 7 tradition in the *Similitudes* demonstrates a process found in other Jewish texts and in the Christian use of the Son of Man imagery.

---

8.   Gabriel also has the appearance of a human in Dan. 8.15. Daniel is called 'son of man' by Gabriel in 8.17.

9.   A similar role seems to be played by Michael in Dan. 10.13, 21; 12.1.

10.   Nickelsburg, 'Son of Man', p. 138.

11.   In a similar scene from the third century BCE a human figure (Enoch) is presented before the heavenly throne (*1 En.* 14.8-24).

In the *Similitudes* the Son of Man has become a heavenly figure who represents the righteous and chosen ones in their warfare with the kings and the mighty. The description of this figure is a composite one drawn from three streams of Old Testament tradition: Daniel 7; Isaiah 11; and Psalm 2, with Isaiah 42, 49, 52–53. A variety of images coalesce in this individual: he is the heavenly Son of Man; he is the Davidic king; he is the Servant of the Lord. This Son of Man is pre-existent (*1 En.* 48.3), and he bears other traits of wisdom. Through the spirit which he bears he will judge correctly *(1 En.* 49.1-4). His judgment vindicates the persecuted righteous, and they subsequently enjoy eternal life in the presence of the Son of Man (*1 En.* 62–63). A surprising revelation may occur in ch. 71, which is probably a late addition to the *Similitudes*. Here Enoch ascends to the heavenly realm, where he comes before the Lord of the Spirits. There an angel addresses him as 'son of man'. *If* this greeting identifies Enoch with the heavenly judge,[12] then the reign of the heavenly Son of Man is preceded by his earthly travail. This earthly identity of the Son of Man would be veiled until his heavenly judgment. In this manner the images of Daniel 7 are developed into a clear apocalyptic vision of the heavenly Son of Man who comes with judgment and vindication, perhaps after a period of earthly trials.

The Wisdom of Solomon, dated around the beginning of the common era, shares important aspects of this tradition. Although the Son of Man title is never used, Wisdom of Solomon 1–5 speaks of the Righteous One who is persecuted and killed by rich and powerful opponents. This righteous person is subsequently vindicated in the heavenly realms, much to the surprise of his opponents. In distinction from the Enoch tradition this figure is human throughout, and he typifies the oppressed righteous. His vindication is a personal reward given by God, and he does not initiate judgment against his oppressors. This figure is less a heavenly judge than a model of the ultimate vindication of the righteous.

The echoes of the Daniel tradition are also found in *4 Ezra*, dated from the end of the first century CE. The visions in *4 Ezra* 11–12 and 13 borrow extensively from the vision of Daniel 7. The four beasts reappear, with the fourth being the most powerful and arrogant (*4 Ezra* 11.36-46). This beast is similarly burned (*4 Ezra* 12.3). The text itself

---

12. E. Isaac, '1 (Ethiopic Apocalypse of) Enoch', *OTP*, I, pp. 5-89 (50), argues that this phrase is distinct from the term applied to the heavenly Son of Man. He thinks the phrase applied to Enoch means 'a masculine person'.

connects the vision to Daniel (*4 Ezra* 12.11). The image of a deliverer is prominent in this vision. A figure like a lion is roused from the forest, but this character speaks in a human voice in behalf of the Most High (*4 Ezra* 11.37-38). This figure is the Messiah, the offspring of David whom God has kept for the end of days (*4 Ezra* 12.31-32). He will serve as the judge of the wicked oppressors and as the deliverer of the righteous remnant (*4 Ezra* 12.32-34).

One with the figure of a man is also prominent in the vision of *4 Ezra* 13. This figure is frequently called 'a man' (*4 Ezra* 13.3, 5, 12, 25, 51), but he is addressed by the Most High as 'my Son' (*4 Ezra* 13.32, 37, 52). He has been kept by the Most High for many ages, and he will deliver the righteous (*4 Ezra* 13.25-26). He will judge and destroy the wicked through the law (*4 Ezra* 13.38), and he will reconstitute the lost tribes of Israel (*4 Ezra* 13.39-50). In this manner *4 Ezra* extends the concepts of Daniel 7 and addresses social and political events near the end of the first century CE.

Further echoes of this tradition are found in *2 Baruch*, also dated near the end of the first century CE. The judicial role of the figure from Daniel 7 is acted out against the fourth beast (*2 Bar.* 36–39). Various aspects of this figure make him more than human: he will have a glorious appearance (*2 Bar.* 29–30), he is the agent of universal judgment (*2 Bar.* 53–74), and he appears in the image of lightning (2 Bar. 53.9, 12; see 70.7-10; 72.1-7). Two traits of this figure are significant in view of the developing tradition: he is frequently described as 'my anointed one', and he is more than a human. The messianic title represents an expansion of Danielic tradition, and the transcendent nature is an expansion of the Jewish idea of kingship.[13]

This line of evidence seems to indicate a rather strong Jewish tradition of a heavenly judge and deliverer by the end of the first century CE. Nickelsburg describes this as 'a common model that was composed of elements from Israelite traditions about the Davidic king, the Deutero-Isaianic servant/chosen one, and the Danielic "son of man"'.[14] This tradition is marked by its conflation of various Jewish traditions and by its unique address to situations of persecution. The developing Jewish eschatology evidenced in these texts provides an important framework against which to read the Son of Man Christologies of the New Testament. Nonetheless scholarship must reckon with the very real

13. So Nickelsburg, 'Son of Man', p. 141.
14. Nickelsburg, 'Son of Man', p. 141.

possibility that use of the Son of Man to refer to a coming heavenly judge is first found with Jesus and/or the early Church.

The Literary Foreground

The background of the Son of Man title is diverse and complex. Linguistically the concept may provide a generic or indefinite reference to a human, it may be used in direct address, or it may refer to the speaker. A range of apocalyptic imagery drawn from various sources seems to coalesce near the end of the first century CE. New Testament images which speak of the Son of Man as a future judge belong in some way to this developing tradition. The hidden sojourn of the Son of Man as the earthly Jesus *may* have a parallel in *1 Enoch*. Nowhere in the pre-Christian material does suffering play an explicit role in the story of the Son of Man. The Gospel of Mark stands within this developing complex of tradition, yet it makes its own distinctive use of the Son of Man title.

Distribution

The Son of Man title is the most frequent of the christological images in the Gospel of Mark. It occurs some 14 times and is found throughout the narrative (2.10, 28; 8.31, 38; 9.9, 12, 31; 10.33, 45; 13.36; 14.21 [twice],41, 62). The Son of Man title belongs almost exclusively to the last half of the narrative (chs. 8–16); only the sayings in 2.10, 28 employ this term in the opening half. Thus, the Son of Man title is a frequent and widespread image which increases as the story line approaches the passion account.

Association

Two conflicting themes are connected to the Son of Man title in the Gospel of Mark. One sequence creates a clear association with the power and judgment of the Son of Man. The display of this authority belongs largely to the future. The Son of Man will be raised from the dead (8.31; 9.9, 31; 10.33). He will come with the angels in the glory of his Father (8.38).[15] The Son of Man will be seen coming in the clouds with great power and glory, and he will gather the elect from the corners of creation (13.26-27). The Son of Man will be seen seated at the right hand of power and coming with the clouds of heaven (14.62).

---

15. Thus, the Son of Man is also the Son of God.

In two instances (2.10, 28), the power of the Son of Man seemingly belongs to the present age. In Mk 2.10 the Son of Man has authority to forgive sins upon the earth. In 2.28 he is lord over the sabbath and its demands. While both verses could refer to the future reign of the Son of Man, the present activity of Jesus provides the most likely point of reference. The Gospel of Mark thus posits a clear association between the Son of Man title and images of power and judgment. While this connection belongs mostly to the future (8.38; 9.9; 13.26; 14.62), its impact is already at work in the present (2.20, 28).

A contrasting association emerges around the Son of Man title in Mk 8.31; 9.12, 31; 10.33, 45; 14.21 (twice), 41. The Son of Man must, of necessity, suffer much and be rejected by the religious leaders (8.31). The Scriptures foretell the suffering and belittling of the Son of Man (9.12). The Son of Man will be handed over to people who will kill him (9.31). In Jerusalem the Son of Man will be betrayed to the religious leaders, who will condemn him to death and hand him over to the nations (10.33). Even the Son of Man did not come to be served, but to serve and to give his life (10.45). In fulfillment of the Scriptures, the Son of Man is handed over and goes up to his death (14.21 [twice]). At the end of his prayers in Gethsemane the Son of Man is handed over to sinners (14.41). These scenes pose a stark contrast to the power and judgment of the Son of Man: he has come to serve, to suffer and to die.

Confirmation
The narrative employs various techniques to affirm the Son of Man title. First, the imagery is drawn from the Old Testament. The foundation of the Son of Man image upon the text of Dan. 7.13 validates the title in the Gospel of Mark. Other aspects of this characterization echo the Old Testament. The Son of Man is God's Son (8.38). His commission to serve (10.45) may echo the Servant psalms from Isaiah, as does his suffering. His advent is preceded by the fulfillment of Scripture (13.24-27). Through these and other techniques the Son of Man imagery operates against the backdrop of the Old Testament.

Secondly, the Son of Man sayings and predictions belong only to Jesus. Placing this title exclusively on the lips of the narrative's most reliable witness further authenticates the title.

Thirdly, the Son of Man image is connected to other titles. The Son of Man who will sit at the right hand of power (14.62) has been designated to rule by God (Ps. 110.1; Mk 12.35-37). He is David's Lord

(12.35-37). The Son of Man is the Messiah, the Son of God (8.38; 14.61-62).

Fourthly, the Son of Man title is connected uniquely to the identity and mission of Jesus. Within the Gospel of Mark, the Son of Man title is never a confessional statement, either on the lips of Jesus or any other character. Further, the title is never used directly of Jesus in the Gospel of Mark. Nonetheless, the narrative identification of the Son of Man with Jesus is clear. Thus, the Gospel of Mark confirms the Son of Man title as a mysterious but valid description which belongs appropriately to the mission and identity of Jesus.

Development

Complex character traits surround the Son of Man title. On the one hand clear lines of application are drawn. The Son of Man is an authority figure whose future coming is marked by power, glory and judgment (8.38; 9.9; 13.26; 14.62). His authority is already present (2.10, 28). He is the embodiment of the apocalyptic vision of Daniel. The way of the Son of Man upon the earth is marked by service, suffering, and death (8.31; 9.12, 31; 10.33, 45; 14.21 [twice], 41). The Son of Man title is associated with other titles—Lord (2.28), Christ (14.61-62), Son of God (8.28; 14.61-62)—and with the work of Jesus.

On the other hand the Son of Man image remains shrouded in mystery. Neither the narrator nor any character confesses Jesus as the Son of Man. Jesus never directly and unambiguously applies the term to himself. The conflict between lowliness and power remains unresolved, as does the tension between future and present. Within this text the Son of Man remains an elusive character.

Several lines of development may be demonstrated around the Son of Man title. These narrative techniques do not unravel the mystery of the Son of Man, but they do provide keys for understanding the powerful impact of the Son of Man figure upon the story of Jesus.

First, the Gospel of Mark connects the mystery of the Son of Man to the ministry of Jesus. While Son of Man is never a confessional title in the Gospel of Mark, the narrative identification of the Son of Man with Jesus is certain. The forgiving authority of the Son of Man is connected to Jesus' own pronouncement of forgiveness (2.1-12).[16] Likewise, the

---

16. It is quite likely that ἀφίενται is a divine passive which refers to God's forgiveness. In that case Jesus is the one who announces *God's* forgiveness, and the

authority of the Son of Man over sabbath requirements is linked to Jesus' own restructuring of sabbath piety (2.23-28). In a similar manner, resurrection is a fate common to both Jesus and the Son of Man (8.31; 9.12, 31; 10.33; 16.1-8). Through these connections the destiny of the Son of Man and of Jesus coincide.

More significantly, the passion of Jesus belongs to the mystery of the Son of Man. On his way to Jerusalem Jesus predicts the passion of the Son of Man (8.31; 9.12, 31; 10.33). In the face of abandonment and death Jesus speaks of the betrayal of the Son of Man (14.21 [twice], 41). The ministry of Jesus occasions the saying concerning the service and death of the Son of Man (10.45). Consequently the death of Jesus is the passion of the Son of Man.

Thus, the identity of the Son of Man is tied carefully to the ministry and passion of Jesus. This narrative technique creates a crucial hermeneutical key: the mysterious power of the Son of Man is explicated in the deeds of Jesus' life and death.

Secondly, the Gospel of Mark connects the mystery of the Son of Man to the working of Yahweh. The throne of power belongs to the Son of Man (14.62), but God alone designates the one who rules from this position (Ps. 110.1; Mk 12.35-37). This rule belongs to the future and to the work of Yahweh, who will place all opponents beneath the feet of God's chosen ruler. Thus, the Son of Man title, like the κύριος title, holds a theological point of reference in priority over its christological imagery.[17] Consequently, the Son of Man is not an isolated conquerer, but the sovereign designated to rule by Yahweh. He will come, not in his own name, but in the glory of the Father (8.38).

Thirdly, the Gospel of Mark connects the mystery of the Son of Man to the future. There is a mystery which remains until the raising of the Son of Man. His resurrection is given as a prophecy of things to come (8.31; 9.31; 10.33). The appearance of the Son of Man is a future event (ὄψονται in 13.26, ὄψεσθε in 14.62). His judgment belongs to the future age (8.38; 13.37). He is seated at the right hand of God, but he awaits God's overcoming of all enemies (Ps. 110.1; Mk 12.36; 14.62). Though the Son of Man exercises authority over sin and sabbath, his reign is yet to come.

---

exclusive nature of God is maintained. On the priestly nature of this act, see Chapter 5. A similar expression may be found at Qumran in 4QPrNab.

17. See Chapter 14.

Finally, the contrasting images of lowliness and power which circulate around the Son of Man title are merged within the narrative itself. A hint of their union is given in the passion predictions (8.31; 9.31; 10.32-34) when the suffering and death of the Son of Man are followed by his resurrection. This linkage of power and passion emerges most clearly in Mk 14.61-62. In the context of his trial and condemnation to death (14.53-65), Jesus clearly acknowledges his identity as Christ and Son of God (14.62).[18] To the stark ἐγώ εἰμι of 14.62 is added the Son of Man prophecy. Here the ruling imagery of Psalm 110 is combined with the coming imagery of Daniel 7 to create a focused image of power and judgment. Significantly, this stark vision of the Son of Man belongs precisely to the context of Jesus' passion. Thus, the narrative links the contrasting sides of the Son of Man precisely in the condemnation and death of Jesus.

Effect
The hermeneutical impact of these narrative patterns is significant. The Son of Man title is embedded within the fabric of the text, yet it remains a mystery. The term is frequent, but it is given little direct explication. Images of power and lowliness conflict within the story. Son of Man never serves as a confessional title in the Gospel of Mark. This title does not frame the larger story and control its elements in the way the Christ and Son of God titles do. Consequently the Son of Man title is a part of the story, yet its key role is to point beyond the story. It is a connected mystery, an embedded secret whose depth and extent exceed the reach of the story line. The keys to this title lie in God's power to reign, in the deeds of Jesus, and in the events of the future.

The Son of Man thus becomes an indefinable yet inescapable sign that opens up the scope of the narrative. The narrative itself cannot provide the final definition of the Son of Man. This mystery belongs to the realms that the narrative can only designate, but never delineate—to the sovereignty of God and to the mystery of the future. At the same time this unfathomable mystery is embedded in the story of Jesus, in whom the power and passion of the Son of Man coincide. Thus, the story is thrown open to new depths of mystery and to the uncharted course of

---

18. The assertion by Cullmann that the answer is ambiguous is to be rejected. The use of ἐγώ εἰμι invokes the Old Testament name of Yahweh as witness to the identity of Jesus.

the future. The Son of Man title is as much a christological question
and challenge as it is an answer or a description.

Conclusion

The mystery of the Son of Man as it is embedded in the story of Jesus
explores the depths of the sovereignty of God and exposes the narrative
to the claim of the future. This move exceeds the plot line, and the story
is opened to a new dimension of power and to a new era of hope. This
transaction proves particularly effective in view of Jesus' death. While
the other Gospels narrate the victory of Jesus over death (Mt. 28.16-20;
Lk. 24.13; Jn 20.11–21.25), the Gospel of Mark transcends the death of
Jesus through its Son of Man imagery. As a consequence the suffering
and death of Jesus become more than human crime or catastrophe. The
death of Jesus, as his whole story, is taken up into the sovereign power
of God and into the unfinished narrative of the future. Operating within
the realm of the narrative, the Son of Man title also becomes the vehicle
through which the narrative moves beyond itself and its own limita-
tions.

Attention to the formal traits of this narrative presentation does not
unravel the linguistic or historical problems underlying the Son of Man
title, nor can it clarify the place of this term on the lips of Jesus. Formalistic analysis does, however, clarify the dramatic impact of this
image upon the Christology of this Gospel. While the Son of Man title
emerges as a description shaped and empowered by the moves of this
narrative, this title ultimately exceeds the power of the narrative to
clarify and to complete. The Son of Man title bequeaths to this Gospel
an unsolved mystery and an unfinished tale. As a consequence, the last,
disastrous events of the story line provide neither the final acts nor the
final verdict of this drama. Only the advent of the Son of Man, promised in the story of Jesus, can complete this narrative.

Chapter 14

LORD

But she answered and said to him, 'Lord, even the little dogs beneath the table eat from the crumbs of the children' (Mk 7.28).

The background of the term Lord proves diverse and elusive. Because of this, the transformation of the term into a christological title is difficult to explain. The use of this title within the literary world of the Gospel of Mark proves equally complex.

The Historical Background

The title Lord is used of gods and/or rulers in Oriental thought, in Egypt, in classical Greece, and in Hellenism.[1] Within the Roman culture the term was applied to the emperor, but initially in situations not related to cultic or religious activity.[2] The use within Roman life seems to reflect its importation from the eastern areas of the empire. While the term was accepted by the emperors with some hesitancy, its usage developed in the last century BCE. By the time of Domitian its role in the western empire seems fixed.[3] Thus, the term likely was embedded

---

1. W. Förster, 'κύριος', *TDNT*, III, pp. 1034-58, especially pp. 1047-54, cites examples from these areas.

2. Förster, 'κύριος', pp. 1054-58.

3. Hahn, *Titles*, pp. 69-70, traces this development: '...an eastern origin is indisputable. Through Alexander the Great, the Seleucids and the Ptolemies, court ceremonial and the apotheosis of the ruler gradually penetrated to the west. In the first and second centuries B.C. kyrios is found only in the east. But already with Caesar and especially with Augustus, veneration of the ruler gained ground even in the west. No doubt Augustus himself, as Tiberius after him, shunned the ascription to himself of the kyrios title, for the whole oriental conception of the ruler was alien to ancient Roman feeling; in any case, in the eastern part of the empire such veneration of the emperor was suffered. However, from Caligula and with increasing rapidity, from Nero onwards, the kyrios title and the cult of the emperor became

within all aspects of the Roman emperor's office by the end of the first century BCE.

The image of lordship was widespread in the Greco-Roman world into which Christianity moved in the last half of the first century CE. Here it could refer to human authority, to respectful address, or to a divine status. For many scholars this line of development explains the entrance of Lord into the christological descriptions of the early Church: the unique status and authority of the risen Jesus are expressed in language and concepts borrowed from the world of Hellenism.[4]

Others have sought to explain the Christian confession that 'Jesus is Lord' in terms of a Hebraic background mediated through Palestinian Christianity.[5] The key to this argument lies in the question of whether κύριος was employed as a term of description for Yahweh in pre-Christian contexts. The most obvious proof of this seems to lie in the fact that the Septuagint uses κύριος to translate the name of God in the Old Testament. While this evidence seems convincing, it must be noted that the use of κύριος for Yahweh can be found only in Christian copies of the Septuagint dating from the fourth century CE and later.[6] Pre-Christian translations of the Old Testament that are available use Hebrew characters, not κύριος, to replace the name of Yahweh. If this pattern is consistent, then a non-Hebraic origin for the use of κύριος for Yahweh would be likely.[7] Recent evidence seems to point the other way, however. Within pre-Christian Palestine, Jews probably spoke of Yahweh in Hebrew as *'ādōn*, in Aramaic as *mārê* and *māryā*, and in Greek as κύριος.[8]

---

prevalent in the west also, and with Domitian, both no doubt became finally established.'

4.   Bousset, *Kyrios Christos*, esp. pp. 119-152; Bultmann, *Theology of the New Testament*, I, pp. 51-53; 121-33.

5.   So, e.g., G. Dalman, *The Words of Jesus Considered in the Light of Post-Biblical Jewish Writings and the Aramaic Language* (trans. D. Kay; Edinburgh: T. & T. Clark, 1902), pp. 324-31; Cullmann, *Christology*, pp. 195-237; E. Schweizer, *Lordship and Discipleship* (London: SCM Press, 1960 [1955]), pp. 56-60; 98-116.

6.   The evidence for this is discussed by Conzelmann, *An Outline*, pp. 83-84.

7.   Fitzmyer, *Luke*, pp. 200-204, discusses these possibilities.

8.   Fitzmyer, *Luke*, p. 202. Fitzmyer believes that 'It was probably formulated in Greek by the "Hellenists" and in Aramaic or Hebrew by the "Hebrews" among them'.

Within the texts of the Hebrew Old Testament, a tetragrammaton is used for the name of God. Because of reticence to speak the name of God (and perhaps to mispronounce or misuse it), the tetragrammaton JHVH began to be replaced with *Adonai*, which was taken from the realm of secular usage where it refers to a master or owner (Gen. 19.2). This change marks a sharp transition in which the tetragrammaton, which represents the exclusive identity of Israel's God, is replaced by a common description of ruling power. The key problem is when this transition occured. *Adonai* was already the typical Jewish designation for God by the first century BCE, but did the transition occur earlier? Of central importance is the question of whether this transition from JHVH to *Adonai* predated the Septuagint. If so, then the use of κύριος in the Septuagint may represent no more than a translation of *Adonai*. If not, then it is likely in the Septuagint that JHVH is first translated by a common description of authority. The key issue at stake here is at what point the decisive step was taken to employ a common term from secular usage to refer to the God of Israel.

While the issue of the Septuagintal use of κύριος cannot be answered in definitive terms, it is likely that both *Adonai* and κύριος were used in Palestinian and Diaspora Judaism prior to the Christian era. The pseude-pigraphal writings of Judaism seem to confirm this. The *Psalms of Solomon* employ two lines of description for God: κύριος, ὁ κύριος and κύριε on the one hand, θεός and ὁ θεός on the other hand. Josephus also knows the use of κύριος for *Adonai* (*Ant.* 5.121). He uses κύριε of God in a prayer (*Ant.* 20.90) and in a citation (*Ant.* 13.68). While Philo found the terms θεός and κύριος alongside each other in the Septu-agint, he created an allegorical distinction between the terms: he saw κύριος in reference to kingly authority and θεός in relation to gracious power.[9] *Psalms of Solomon* 17.32 speaks of the Lord Messiah (χριστὸς κύριος), and this may represent the best reading of the texts.[10]

At some point in the history of development the Greek term κύριος, which points to secular authority and is a term of respect in personal address, was used in reference to Yahweh. This transition—whether translating a prior Hebrew transition or making this transition itself—marks a major conceptual shift: the rarely spoken and exclusive name

9. Förster, 'κύριος', pp. 1082-83.

10. The evidence is discussed by Wright, 'Psalms of Solomon', pp. 667-68. A similar form is found in *Pss. Sol.* 18.7.

of Yahweh is interpreted and replaced by a term of authority in widespread use. At whatever linguistic stage this transition occurred, the result is similar: it now becomes extremely difficult to interpret the use of κύριος and related terms when they are applied to other figures—particularly to Jesus.

The Literary Foreground

The use of the Lord title (κύριος) in the Gospel of Mark stands within this complex line of development. External factors prove of limited help in delineating this use. Formalist narrative analysis helps to clarify the role of the Lord title, at least within the world of this Gospel. Through this analysis further light may be shed on the wider use of the Lord title in early Christianity.

Distribution, Association, Confirmation

The κύριος (Lord) title is connected to Jesus only in Mk 7.28 and in secondary readings of 9.24.[11] In both instances the term is ambiguous. Although 7.28 and 9.24 each relate a plea for divine help, κύριος may mean 'sir' or 'master' in both cases. Probably the term is one of respect more than reverence. Here theological or christological images remain, at best, implicit in the address of Jesus as Lord. The narrative strategy neither negates nor develops the term in relation to Jesus' identity.

Development

The formal strategy at work in the Gospel of Mark provides a complex backdrop against which to interpret the κύριε address in Mk 7.28. Four distinct lines of usage may be identified.

First, in the Gospel of Mark, Lord refers primarily to God. This image is made clear in the first usage in 1.3: taken from Isa. 40.3, the citation refers explicitly to Yahweh. Mark 5.19 probably refers to the healing power of Yahweh, not Jesus. This ambiguity is clarified in D(1241), where κύριος is replaced by θεός. The monotheistic focus of Lord might also be present in Mk 11.3, though the identity of the donkey's κύριος is uncertain.

The reference to God becomes clear in Mk 11.9, which cites Ps. 118.25. Any christological association is blocked by the role of Jesus as the one who comes in the name of the Lord. A similar pattern is found

---

11. D G θ it sy[s].

in Mk 12.10-11. The κύριος of 12.11 is taken from Ps. 118.22 and refers to Yahweh. The christological focus is to be found in the λίθον, the stone once rejected but now made the keystone. All of this happens in the presence of the Lord, that is, Yahweh (Mk 12.11).

In a similar way Mk 12.29-30 defines Lord through Old Testament images. Here the Shema of Deut. 6.4-5 is invoked. In Mk 12.29 the identity of κύριος has a clear monotheistic reference in ὁ θεός. Mark 12.30 echoes this use. Mark 12.36 also invokes this Old Testament understanding: citing Psalm 110, Yahweh is the κύριος who addresses David's κύριος. The reference in Mk 13.20 also follows this pattern; the limiting of eschatological woes points to the Lord of creation, and thus to Yahweh.

So, numerous passages employ κύριος in reference to Yahweh. The monotheistic focus is made explicit in the Old Testament citations (1.3; 11.9; 12.11, 29-30, 36) and is reinforced by other images. As a consequence, Lord refers in the Gospel of Mark primarily to Yahweh, the creator and the one God of Israel.

A second line of usage employs Lord in a common, secular manner to refer to an earthly master. This is the likely meaning of Mk 2.28, where the Son of Man is designated κύριος of the sabbath, though deeper implications lie close at hand. Mark 11.3 may be a common reference to the owner or master of the donkey. In 12.9 κύριος refers to the owner or ruler of a vineyard.

The construction in Mk 12.36-37 is unusual. While the first Lord refers to Yahweh, a second figure is addressed by Yahweh. This figure is designated as 'my lord' (κυρίῳ μου). The questions of Jesus in 12.35, 37 clarify this image: David calls the Messiah his master.

The master image is taken up in the midst of the eschatological discourse in Mk 13.35. Here Jesus refers to the master of the household. This term is employed in direct address to Jesus in 7.28 and in a variant reading of 9.24. Here the term may be translated as a vocative which expresses respect and carries the meaning of 'sir' or 'master', though the christological meaning lies close at hand.[12]

Thus, a second group of passages in the Gospel of Mark draws the meaning of κύριος from its common use as a term of authority or respect. While these terms are open to christological reinterpretion, their primary focus is secular.

---

12. In a similar way the German 'Herr' is polite address, but may also be used of God.

Thirdly, a number of passages combine these two images by employ-ing the earthly master as a metaphor for God. The ambiguity of Mk 11.3 may be read in this manner. The donkey is needed by its master. Because the earthly owner is never identified, the κύριος of 11.3 is open to interpretation as a theological metaphor or even as a christo-logical metaphor.

The lord of the vineyard in 12.9 is easily understood as an image for Yahweh. The Old Testament figure of Israel as the vineyard of God (Isa. 5.1-10, esp. 5.7) lies close at hand. The abuse of the servants in 12.4 recalls the fate of the Baptist (6.27). The reference to the Beloved Son (12.6) invokes the image of Jesus (1.11; 9.7). Thus, the reader is encouraged to see the parable as an allegory of Israel's relationship with Yahweh. In a similar manner, the lord of the household in Mk 13.35 is a transparent image. This reference may be interpreted either as a theological metaphor or as a christological image.

Thus, a selected group of verses uses the κύριος imagery as a metaphor. In these instances the secular master of the household, the vineyard, the livestock may be taken as an image of God.

Fourth and finally, a single passage employs κύριος in explicit ref-erence to the Messiah. In Psalm 110 Yahweh designates one who will sit at the right hand while Yahweh exercises authority. The citation in Mk 12.36 refers to Yahweh as κύριος (ὁ κύριος in ℵ A L W θ Ψ 092 b f[1.13] 𝔐) and to the designated ruler as κυρίῳ μου. While the Old Testament context does not identify the figure, the passage is inter-preted in Mk 12.35-37 in christological terms: David is understood to refer to the messiah as 'my lord'. This interpretation provides the basis for the unanswered christological riddle posed in 12.37: 'David himself calls him lord; how then is he his son?' While this reference is clearly christological, the debate remains abstract: Jesus does nothing to ex-plicitly connect this image to his own ministry, nor does the narrator.

Thus, the κύριος title is developed through four distinct patterns in the Gospel of Mark. Its primary use may echo the Greek Old Testament and has reference to Yahweh as the one God of Israel. A second use employs the secular sense of κύριος as 'master', 'ruler', 'sir'. A few passages combine these images and employ the secular κύριος as a metaphor for God's rule. A single passage reads the κύριος figure of Psalm 110 as a reference to the Messiah, but it does not attach this image explicitly to Jesus.

Effect

This narrative strategy has a profound effect upon the role of the Lord title. In this Gospel, as in the ethos of the Old Testament, Lord refers first and foremost to God. The primary focus of the term is monotheistic, as the citation of the Shema demonstrates. The sharing of the title in Psalm 110/Mk 12.36-37 is at the instigation of Yahweh. This usage of κύριος may be drawn from the linguistic world of the Septuagint.

Running counter to this theological use of κύριος as the exclusive Lord of Israel and of all creation is the common use of κύριος to mean an earthly authority. This use of the term is drawn from the linguistic realm of secular Hellenistic thought. This term of authority is used primarily of property owners, though it is applied as well to Jesus (7.28; 9.24) and to the Son of Man (2.28). The narrative employs the secular κύριος on occasion as a metaphor for Yahweh. This application is typical of the parabolic use of secular images to clarify the sacred.[13]

Significantly, the Gospel of Mark combines these two images (sacred and secular) only as metaphors, only once as a clear christological image (12.35-37), and never with explicit reference to the identity and mission of Jesus. Thus, κύριος is a clear messianic title only in 12.36-37, where it is not directly attached to Jesus. In the Gospel of Mark the Church confession that 'Jesus is Lord' is never directly embraced. Instead, a more oblique and indirect connection is drawn between the theological and christological aspects of the Lord title.

In the Gospel of Mark the religious aspects of κύριος belong to God, though Yahweh may designate one to rule (Psalm 110/Mk 12.35-37). This agent is the Messiah (12.35, 37), a term elsewhere attached explicitly to Jesus (1.1, 34; 8.29; 14.61). Thus, the reader may easily infer, within this narrative world, that Jesus the Messiah is the Lord of David who is designated to rule at Yahweh's right hand. Significantly, this rule belongs to the future time when Yahweh will set all opponents beneath the feet of the designated ruler. Consequently Jesus may be understood as the messianic Lord whose future rule will be established by Yahweh.

A similar implication is present in Mark 13. The lord of the household in 13.35 provides a clear image of one who will come in judgment. While the coming of Yahweh is a primary Old Testament image,[14] another figure lies closer at hand within this narrative. At the end of the

13. See Mk 12.1-12; 13.28.
14. Zech. 14.5; Mal. 4.5.

eschatological woes the Son of Man will come with power and glory to gather the elect (13.26-27). The clear designation of Jesus as the Son of Man (Mk 14.21 [twice], 41) opens the way to a christological connection: the κύριος who will come at the end of the age is none other than Jesus, the Son of Man.

These two connections are united in Mk 14.62. In the face of questions about his identity as Christ and Son of God (14.61), the reply of Jesus is unambiguous: ἐγώ εἰμι (14.62). The answer of Jesus unites the images of Psalm 110 and Daniel 7: the Son of Man will be seen at the right hand of power, and he will come with the clouds of heaven. While Jesus does not expressly identify himself as this Son of Man, the narrative leaves no doubt about this connection (Mk 14.21 [twice] ,41). Thus, the coming Lord who will rule at God's initiative is none other than Jesus.

Significantly, this connection is both practical and futuristic. No ontology is created to equate the essence of Jesus with that of God. No doctrine of pre-existence is developed. Theology is not absorbed into Christology, and the exclusive divinity of Yahweh is maintained. Jesus will rule as Lord only because God has so designated. It is God who will set the enemies beneath the feet of the chosen Lord. Beyond this, his rule belongs to the future: he will come to reign at the end of the age.

The Gospel of Mark thus points to the lordship of Jesus, but only indirectly as an existential experience and never as an absorption of the identity of Yahweh. While much of the early Church confessed that 'Jesus is Lord' and struggled to work out the theological implications of that confession, the Gospel of Mark employs a different paradigm: the designated κύριος seated at God's right hand and coming to rule at the close of the age will be none other than Jesus.

This complex linkage of the work of Jesus to the exclusive identity of God allows other narrative connections. In retrospect, the future reign of Jesus may be seen in various passages. The one who will come as Lord may be understood indirectly as Lord of the sabbath (2.28), as the Lord who heals (5.19), as the Lord who has need of the donkey (11.3). Most significantly, the polite address of 7.28 (and 9.24) may be seen as a foreshadow. The reader knows that the κύριος who heals the hurting children will one day rule over all his enemies.

Thus, the Gospel of Mark employs the κύριος title to generate a delicate and complex christological image. Yahweh is the Lord who rules over Israel and over all creation. Earthly masters may serve as metaphors and parables for the rule of God. Yahweh has designated a messianic Lord seated at the right hand. This κύριος-designate is the Son of Man who is to come. This coming Lord to whom God will subject all enemies is none other than Jesus. Through a careful retrospective reading, this future lordship may be seen in various images from Jesus' life and ministry.

Conclusion

The Gospel of Mark employs unique strategies to construct the κύριος image and to employ it in naming Jesus. This use of the Lord title provides an important bridge within the christological developments of early Christianity. Reflected within this characterization is the primitive concept of Jesus as the future agent of salvation. This early Christology is found in different literary stages and is attached to various titles.[15] Initially this concept is a transformation of the Day of Yahweh imagery of the Old Testament (2 Pet. 3.10-13).

Various aspects of this primitive concept are developed within the New Testament. The idea of the initiation of salvation or of the completion of a salvation already begun is central to this thought. The status of Jesus at the right hand of God or in heaven is noted. Some particular name or office of Jesus is emphasized. The position and status of Jesus are usually connected to his resurrection. In most instances Jesus is already active in his new office. This reality may already be experienced by believers, but will be universally known in the future.

The treatment of the Lord title in the Gospel of Mark provides an early form of this primitive Christology. The κύριος-designate who is seated at the right hand of God is the coming Son of Man, who is identified in this Gospel as Jesus. Thus, the Gospel of Mark presents a primitive understanding of the lordship of Jesus which maintains the exclusive nature of God and the eschatological nature of salvation.

---

15. Traces of this Christology may be seen in 1 Pet. 3.21-22; 5.4; Phil. 2.6-11; Col. 3.4; Eph. 4.30; Acts 2.19-21, 32-36; 5.30-31; 7.55; Mk 13.26-27; 14.62. It is linked to the following titles: Shepherd, Lord, Messiah, Leader, Savior, Son of Man. As this Christology develops, the believer's present experience of the Lordship of Jesus is emphasized, usually through the work of the Holy Spirit. The Gospel of Mark stands at a junction between a purely functional and futuristic Christology and the more experiential orientation to the present activity of the risen Jesus.

While the Gospel of Mark does not present Christology and soteri-ology as fully realized concepts, the door is opened to the present experience of the believer. Through the secular and the metaphorical uses of the κύριος title the future lordship of Jesus may be seen at work already. In a similar way the authority of the Son of Man may be present already (Mk 2.10, 28). Mark 16.1-8 may be an invitation for believers to experience Jesus' lordship in Galilee.

Thus, the use of Lord in the Gospel of Mark stands at a crucial juncture in the development of Christology. Through the strategic patterns of this narrative the lordship of Jesus is affirmed in terms that are functional, futuristic, and monotheistic. This Gospel thus avoids the temptations of a Christology which diverges into ontological speculation and impinges upon the identity of Yahweh. On the other hand, the exclusive role of Jesus beyond his earthly activity is articulated, and the present impact of his sovereignty is held in view.

This complex christological balance is constructed within the larger development of these traditions and in dialogue with the historical realities of Jesus' life. At the same time, the unique understanding of Jesus' lordship articulated in the Gospel of Mark is a narrative construction. It is precisely through the formal patterns of this Gospel story that—with care—Jesus is named as Lord.

Chapter 15

CHRIST

'Are you the Christ, the son of the Blessed One?' (Mk 14.61).

The Christ title provides the most frequent description of Jesus in the New Testament and in early Christianity, though most scholars are sceptical that Jesus used this term of himself. This New Testament usage emerges from a long line of development of the term in the Old Testament and in Judaism. When seen within this line of development, the Christ title plays an unusual literary role within the Gospel of Mark.

The Historical Background

The New Testament title of Christ (χριστός) is a translation of the Hebrew *mashiach*. Both terms have their root in verbal forms meaning 'to anoint'. The idea of individuals anointed by God for a special task is widespread in the Old Testament.[1] The most common use is in reference to the king as God's anointed. This description applies primarily to David (1 Sam. 16.3, 12-13; 2 Sam. 2.4, 7; 5.3, 17; 12.7; Ps. 89.20; 1 Chron. 11.3; 14.8). Subsequently the term is used in reference to David's descendants who serve as king (1 Kgs 1.34, 19, 45; 2 Kgs 2.11; 23.20; 2 Sam. 19.11), though others are also anointed (1 Sam. 9.16; 1 Kgs 19.15, 16). The anointing of the king was probably a part of an enthronement ceremony. Yahweh's election and anointing—rather than the physical sonship of Oriental and Egyptian kings—established kingship in Israel. This act is usually accompanied by terms of empowerment, commission and promise. The anointing of David, for example,

---

1.　See W. Grundmann, F. Hesse and A. van der Woude, M. de Jonge, 'χρίω', *TDNT*, IX, pp. 493-580; Fitzmyer, *Luke*, pp. 197-200; H. Conzelmann, *An Outline*, pp. 72-75; Cullmann, *Christology*, pp. 111-36.

is accompanied by the coming of the Spirit of God upon him (1 Sam. 16.13). Cyrus, the Persian king, is likewise called God's anointed (Isa. 45.1).

Priests were also anointed within Israel (Exod. 29.7, 29-30; 40.13; Lev. 6.13; 8.12).[2] This may arise as a postexilic practice initially applied to the high priests. While this anointing carries some sense of empowerment and the continuation of the Davidic heritage, separation and sanctification are also focused. Eventually the practice is understood in terms of cleansing and consecration and is described in reference to all priests (Exod. 28.41; 30.30; 40.15; Lev. 7.36; Num. 3.3).

The Old Testament also tells of prophetic anointing. 1 Kings 19.16 points to a ritual in which Elijah anoints Elisha. In Isa. 61.1 the prophet receives the Spirit of the Lord as a result of anointing by Yahweh. The patriarchs are described as anointed ones and as prophets in Ps. 105.15.

The Old Testament also speaks of the anointing of objects: pillars (Gen. 28.18; 31.13); altars (Exod. 29.36; 40.10; Lev. 8.11; Num. 7.1, 10, 84, 88); the tent of meeting (Exod. 30.26); and other objects. Here the idea of consecration is predominant.

The primary reference of this term to David and his royal descendants connects it to various other images and to the developing hopes for an endtime deliverer. The development of this idea can be traced from various Old Testament contexts. The royal psalms (such as Pss. 2, 21, 89, 110, 132) expect that Yahweh's sovereignty will be expressed through Israel's king. To some extent the existence and the reputation of Yahweh are demonstrated in the success of the king, and thus of Israel. The failure of Israel's monarch thus calls into question the status of Yahweh. The political and spiritual failure of Israel is not, however, seen as permanent. God is expected to intervene through a heroic human figure who will re-establish Israel's political and spiritual strength (Isa. 9.1-7). Jeremiah looks for this Davidic king and calls him by the name 'The Lord is Righteousness' (Jer. 23.5-6). Ezekial expects a period of restoration (Ezek. 36.22-38), and he sees this accomplished through a Davidic king (Ezek. 34.23-24). This hope probably flourished in the postexilic period. Haggai may see Zerubbabel, a descendant of David, in these images (Hag. 2.20-23). Zechariah speaks of two anointed agents of Yahweh (Zech. 4.11-14). This prophecy envisions the peaceful cooperation of priestly and political power within Israel (Zech.

---

2. This is found primarily in the Priestly (P) tradition and in passages such as Lev. 4.3, 5, 16; 6.15; 1 Chron. 29.22.

6.9-14). Various other passages look for the restoration of Israel through a Davidic king (Amos 9.11; Hos. 3.5; Jer. 30.8-9).

This expectation of a Davidic king who will establish Israel as a political power and renew its spiritual condition provides the point of collection for Israel's hopes. These hopes unite several concepts: the king as God's anointed, the Davidic kingship, the king as God's Son. While the term for anointing or annointed one is never directly applied as a title to an eschatological deliverer in the Old Testament,[3] these images provide the basis for the more focused messianic expectations that emerge in the last pre-Christian centuries within Palestinian Judaism.

Such expectations came into sharper focus in the centuries preceeding Christianity. Messianic hopes within this period were far from monolithic, but new levels of clarity and intensity were reached. While the *Testament of the Twelve Patriarchs* seemingly speaks of a messiah on occasion, it is difficult to show that this is an authentic, pre-Christian part of the testaments.[4] Clear expressions are found in the *Psalms of Solomon*, dated in the first century BCE and probably Pharisaic in origin. The title of *Psalm* 18 speaks of the 'Lord Messiah' or of the 'Lord's Messiah'.[5] Two lines of this psalm refer to the Messiah:

> May God cleanse Israel for the day of mercy in blessing,
> for the appointed day when his Messiah will reign
> Blessed are those born in those days,
> to see the good things of the Lord
> which he will do for the coming generation;
> (which will be) under the rod of discipline of the Lord's Messiah [or 'of
>   the Lord Messiah']
> in the fear of his God, in the wisdom of spirit (18.5-7).

Psalms of Solomon 17 refers to the Messiah once (17.32), but the entire psalm describes his work. God is the eternal king of Israel and its Savior (17.1-3). God will exercise this rule through David and his descendants (17.4). Political powers and the sins of the people have

3.   1QSa 2.12 may represent the oldest instance of the absolute use of Messiah as a name, and 4QPatr tends in this direction. These passages are noted by A. van der Woude, 'χρίω', *TDNT*, IX, pp. 517-20, 521-27 (509, 518). The absolute use of Messiah may be found in *Pss. Sol.* 17, 18, 19. Apart from these texts the first instance would be in *Syriac Baruch* and in *4 Esdras*, both of which date after 70 CE.

4.   M. de Jonge, 'χρίω', *TDNT*, IX, pp. 509-17, 521-21 (512-13) discusses this.

5.   Wright, 'Psalms of Solomon', pp. 667-68, 669, argues for a reading of the 'Lord Messiah' in 17.32; 19.7; and in the title of Ps. 18.

intervened, and even nature has turned away (17.5-20). In response to this tragedy, *Psalms of Solomon* 17 prays for the intervention of the Messiah. God will raise up this leader (17.21). He will be king (17.21, 32), Son of David (17.21), and Messiah (17.32). He will crush the enemies of Israel (17.22-25), and he will restore the righteousness of the people (17.26-32). Thus, the *Psalms of Solomon* presents a focused expectation of a leader who will restore Israel, and, unlike earlier texts, it names this figure as the Messiah.

A similar clarity is found in the Qumran writings, though in connection with a different type of messianism. Two messianic figures are expected at the end time: a political Messiah of Israel and a priestly Messiah of Aaron. The priestly Messiah takes precedence over the political Messiah, and both are subordinate to God. These figures are not sharply defined as individuals, but rather play a functional role in the forthcoming reign of God.[6]

Thus, a pattern of growth emerges. Pre-Christian messianic expectation develops in the Old Testament around the promise of a Davidic king and emerges within Judaism in the expectations of *Psalms of Solomon* and the Qumran writings. While political and priestly images are central in these expectations, no monolithic concept of the Messiah dominated pre-Christian thought. Within Judaism messianic expectations continued to develop along a variety of avenues beyond the Second Jewish War (second century CE).[7] O. Cullmann notes the following characteristics of this expected leader:

(1) The Messiah fulfils his task in a purely earthly setting.

(2) According to one view, which we find in the Psalms of Solomon, he introduces the end time; according to an earlier conception, he introduces an interim period. In any case the aeon in which he appears is no longer the present one. This temporal consideration distinguishes the Messiah from the Prophet.

(3) Whether it is of peaceful or warlike character, the work of the Jewish Messiah is that of a political king of Israel. He is the national king of the Jews.

(4) The Jewish Messiah is of royal lineage, a descendant of David. For this reason he also bears the title 'Son of David'.[8]

---

6. Van der Woude, 'χρίω', pp. 517-20.

7. This development may be traced primarily in Ecclus 7, in *2 Baruch*, in *4 Ezra*, in Philo, in Josephus and in the rabbinic writings. These and other texts are discussed in *TDNT*, IX, pp. 509-27.

8. Cullmann, *Christology*, p. 117.

Within Christian circles the messianism of the Old Testament and Judaism was transformed into a Christology focused around Jesus. Ultimately the description of Jesus as the Messiah was absorbed into his name—Jesus Christ.

This survey demonstrates that the development of messianic images in the Old Testament and within Judaism was rarely definitive and never monolithic. As a consequence the religious hopes of first-century Palestine were marked by wide-ranging diversity and ambiguity.

The Literary Foreground

As early Christianity recognized, naming Jesus as the Messiah required further explanation. Consequently their message about Jesus did not simply replicate predefined concepts and images; Christian stories explicated and redefined the titles which they inherited. Clearly titles such as Messiah are appropriated and reconstituted in the process of naming Jesus. While this reformulation of Jewish heritage and tradition has a historical and social framework, it can also be demonstrated within the literary world of Christian texts. Through formalist narrative analysis the metamorphosis[9] of the Christ title may be observed within the Gospel of Mark.

Distribution

The Christ title occurs eight times in the Gospel of Mark in an evenly distributed pattern (1.1, 34; 8.29; 9.41; 12.35; 13.21; 14.61; 15.32). The saying in Mk 9.41 belongs to a sequence on discipleship: a reward is promised to all who aid those who belong to Christ. The use of χριστός in 12.35 and 13.21 deals with Christology in an abstract way with no direct relationship to Jesus: the Messiah is David's Lord (12.35-37), and false messiahs will arise in the future (13.21-23). The reading in 1.34 is clearly secondary.[10] Consequently the Gospel of Mark contains four instances in which the Christ title is applied to Jesus (1.1; 8.29; 14.61; 15.32).

---

9. On the technical aspects of this term, see Broadhead, *Teaching with Authority*, pp. 49-50.

10. While a wide range of manuscripts employ the Christ title in Mk 1.34, this is best explained as a harmonization with Lk. 4.41. It is unlikely that the Gospel of Mark originally had this confession, then omitted it. It is more likely that a scribe added this assertion from Luke.

Association

The Christ title remains, for the most part, an undeveloped term throughout the Gospel of Mark. Jesus is flatly acknowledged as the Christ in 1.1 and 8.29, but little depth or description is given to the title. Mark 1.1 stands alone as a superscription over the entire work, with no direct development of the Christ title and no further mention until 8.29. The confession in 8.29 is neither affirmed nor denied, but it is silenced: 'And he commanded them that they should speak to no one concerning him.' The passion teaching which follows (8.31) seems to explicate the Christ title, but this instruction is associated more directly with the Son of Man title. Mark 14.61 directly poses the question of Jesus' identity: 'Are you the Christ...?' Jesus' answer in 14.62 is unambiguous—'ἐγώ εἰμι [I am]'. Nonetheless, the remainder of the answer evokes the Son of Man title and imagery: 'You shall see the Son of Man seated at the right hand of power and coming with the clouds of heaven.' Mark 15.32 presents a taunt on the lips of the chief priest: 'Let the Christ, the King of Israel, come down now from the cross, in order that we might see and believe.' In each of the four scenes, little is done to define the Christ title or to fill out its significance.

The Gospel of Mark does employ one narrative technique to fill out this title. In each of the four instances the Christ title is associated with other titles. In 1.1 the title is associated with a common name (Jesus) and with an uncommon title (Son of God). The Christ title in 8.29 is posited alongside suggestive images: John the Baptist, Elijah, a prophet (8.28). The question in 14.61 places two titles in apposition: 'Are you the Christ, the Son of the Blessed One?' Similarly, Mk 15.32 derides Jesus by connecting two titles: 'Let the Christ, the King of Israel come down...' While these associations broaden the scope of the Christ title, they do little to enrich its definition.

Thus, the Christ title is posited at four decisive points in the narrative, yet the title itself remains flat and isolated. This ambiguous use of the title may be explained in one of three ways: (1) by a shared understanding with the the reader based on historical events or sociological perception; (2) by an incompetent narrative strategy which employs the term in an inappropriate or shallow manner; (3) by a complex strategy in which the title is not defined from events which lie beyond the narrative or from self-contained elements, but receives its definition from the structures and moves of the story. The development of the Christ title within the Gospel of Mark will point to the third option.

Confirmation

The Gospel of Mark confirms the Christ title as a positive description of Jesus. While the confession in Mk 8.29 is immature and is associated with insufficient alternatives (8.28), no objection or denial is raised to Peter's confession *per se*. Mark 15.32 is a derisive taunt associated with a rejected title—King of the Jews. The failure lies not in the Christ title, however, but in those who fail to see its value in relation to the crucified Jesus.

More significantly, the Gospel of Mark frames the life of Jesus with the Christ title. The opening lines of the narrative confirm Jesus as the Messiah (1.1). The identity of Jesus is presented, but not argued. In a similar way the life of Jesus closes with a clear assertion of his identity as the Christ: 'I am', he replies, invoking the Old Testament name of Yahweh. This unequivocal assertion initiates the process of his death (14.63-64). From beginning to end, the Gospel of Mark confirms the identity of Jesus as the Christ.

Development

The Christ title provides a unique example of the narrative development of titles. The title is a positive one which occurs at decisive stages of the narrative. Its validity is misunderstood by some (8.27-30) and rejected by others (15.32), but the reader is assured of its value (1.1; 14.62). The title is posited without definition as a certain, but flat, reality. The local operations which surround the Christ title do little to enhance its significance. Nonetheless, the Gospel of Mark develops the Christ image as a central element in its characterization of Jesus. This is not done through direct association and expansion of the title, but through a complex, extended narrative technique.

While the Christ title is applied to Jesus at only four points, it controls the flow of the entire account. The Christ title is not so much an event within the story[11] as it is an inclusive frame which guides the whole of the story. The Christ claim provides the primary assumption of the narrative (1.1) at its beginning and the climactic confession of the central character, Jesus, at its end (14.62). Consequently the story can spend little energy defining and repeating this title precisely because the story is framed under the guidance of the Christ title. The story lines serves as commentary and explication upon the Christ title

---

11. Indeed, the secrecy motif in Mk 8.30 and the failure to expand upon the title limit its operation within the story.

which frames the story. Such explication need not invoke the title in order to develop its images. The narrative frame of the Gospel of Mark is controlled by the Christ *title*; the story of the Gospel of Mark defines and develops the Christ *image*. Thus, the narrative framework provides the hermeneutical code which realigns the individual elements of the story.

Various aspects of the narrative demonstrate this constructive strategy. The wonders of Jesus are widely paralleled in the history of religions.[12] Seen in isolation, the miracle accounts can hardly be distinguished from their non-canonical parallels. Not their content but their context qualifies and distinguishes the wonders of Jesus. These acts are a part of his authoritative ministry of proclamation (1.21, 39). They belong to the mission and message of Jesus, the one who announces the Gospel of God (1.14). These miracles are the deeds of the Son of God (1.1, 11) in whom the kingdom of God has drawn near (1.15). These wondrous acts belong to the story of the Christ. In the Gospel of Mark these miracles have become statements of Christology which operate under and explicate the titular claims of Mk 1.1 and 14.62: Jesus is Messiah and Son of God.

In a similar way, the teachings of Jesus have numerous parallels. In addition, the Gospel of Mark says little about the details and content of Jesus' teaching.[13] In this Gospel the teachings of Jesus are distinguished primarily through their connection to Christology. The proclamation of Jesus has its central focus in the announcement of God's gospel (1.14) and the approach of God's kingdom (1.15). While the teachings of Jesus convey intrinsic values, their primary significance emerges within the framework of Jesus' proclamation of God. These teachings carry decisive import because they belong to the story of God's Son and Messiah (1.1). Thus, the teachings of Jesus also become statements of

---

12. See examples cited in L. Bieler, *Theios Anēr: Das Bild des 'Göttlichen Menschen' in Spätantike und Frühchristentum* (Darmstadt: Wissenschaftliche Buchgesellschaft, 1967); P. Fiebig, *Jüdische Wundergeschichten des neutestamentlichen Zeitalters, unter besonderer Berücksichtigung ihres Verhältnisses zum Neuen Testament bearbeitet: Ein Beitrag zum Streit um die 'Christusmythe'* (Tübingen: J.C.B. Mohr, 1911).

13. Apart from the focus of Jesus' instruction on basic themes (the kingdom of God, the passion), the most specific details are given in Mk 10. The paucity of teaching material can be seen through comparision with what is known of the Sayings Tradition.

Christology which operate under and explicate the titular claims of Mk 1.1 and 14.61-62.

The Nazarene imagery confirms this narrative strategy.[14] The Nazarene imagery draws upon no historical background and no intrinsic literary value. Its christological significance emerges through patterns of placement and association within the Gospel of Mark. The value of the Nazarene imagery is a literary value gained wholly from the structure and strategies of the narrative. The Nazarene image has christological significance because of its role in the Gospel story. The conclusion is similar: the Nazarene images are statements of Christology which operate under and explicate the titular claims of Mk 1.1 and 14.61-62: Jesus is Messiah and Son of God.

Thus, the Gospel of Mark employs the Christ title as a frame which motivates and guides the entire account. As a consequence the Christ imagery is developed through every aspect of the Gospel story.

Effect

The impact of this strategy is impressive. Without creating the perception that the Christ title is understood by all and applied frequently to Jesus during his ministry, the Gospel of Mark makes significant use of this imagery.

The framing technique employed by this Gospel provides several interpretive guides. First, this strategy creates the impression that the Christ title is not a frequent component of the story, nor need it be. Secondly, this strategy suggests that every event of the story is an interpretation of the Christ title. By providing the hermeneutical key in the titles which frame the narrative, this Gospel insists that all of Jesus' story is christological. The narrative thus extends an invitation to its consumer: this story is to be attended and observed, read and reread, considered and reconsidered in search of the Christ.

Conclusion

Early Christianity did not define Jesus through preconceived, commonly accepted definitions of Messiah, since no such consensus existed. Quite the opposite occurred: early Christianity interpreted Jewish messianism precisely through their experience of Jesus.[15] The Gospel of Mark pro-

---

14. See Chapter 2.

15. Paul and Luke can speak of suffering and crucifixion as the destiny of the

vides the clearest example of this hermeneutic. Since Messiah is not found in what we know of the Sayings Tradition, the Gospel of Mark articulates the first extensive definition of what it means to be the Messiah of Israel. It does so by means of a complex narrative strategy employed in the naming of Jesus.

Taking a concept which had emerged from the Old Testament and pre-Christian Judaism into a broad field of contrasting and contradictory expectations, the Gospel of Mark frames its story with the amorphuous title of Messiah. Operating within the frame created by this title, the story of Jesus now provides definition and demonstration of what it means to be the Christ.

Thus, the significance of the Christ title is not an external value transported into the world of the narrative. Rather, the parameters of the claim that Jesus is the Christ are negotiated precisely through the formal structures and strategies at work in this Gospel.[16] As a consequence of this narrative transaction the Gospel of Mark puts forward a crucial hermeneutical claim: Jesus now provides the definitive key to the Christ title, and Christology forevermore becomes the story of Jesus.

Messiah, not by reading the Old Testament onto the life of Jesus, but by reading the Old Testament in the light of Jesus (for example, Rom. 8.3; 1 Cor. 15.3; Lk. 24.26, 46; Acts 3.18). The same is true of Hebrews (for example, Heb. 2.10; 10.1-14).

16. This narrative strategy likely reflects a historical reality: Jesus probably did not refer to himself as Messiah and was rarely addressed as such in his lifetime. Nonetheless, the early Church confessed the messianic quality of Jesus' life. He is the Christ because he lived and died as such.

Chapter 16

THE RISEN ONE

'But after I have been raised I will go before you into Galilee' (Mk
14.28).

The naming of Jesus as the Risen One demonstrates the way in which
narrative images may be constructed apart from the explicit use of a
title. This process is usually overlooked, but it constitutes an important
strategy in the naming of Jesus.

The characterization of Jesus as the Risen One is never presented in
titular form in the Gospel of Mark. In each of seven instances the narrative presents an act which is performed upon Jesus. Each instance is
stated in verbal form, but never as a substantive.[1] The three passion
predictions (8.31; 9.31; 10.32-34) end with a prediction of Jesus'
resurrection (ἀναστῆναι in 8.31; ἀναστήσεται in 9.31; 10.34). Jesus
predicts his own resurrection (ἐγερθῆναί) in Mk 14.28. This prediction
is fulfilled in Mk 16.6 (ἠγέρθη). Two further instances are found in the
story of the transfiguration (Mk 9.2-10). The disciples are enjoined to
silence about these events until the raising of the Son of Man from the
dead (9.9), but they do not understand what this raising means (9.10).

Key associations are constructed around this image. In each instance,
with the exception of Mk 9.9, 10, the raising of Jesus is connected
explicitly to his violent death. Each of the three passion predictions
describes the abuse and torture Jesus will endure, followed by prediction of his death. The prophecy of Mk 14.28 follows upon the citation
of Zech. 13.7: 'I will strike the shepherd and the sheep shall be scattered' (Mk 14.27). The proclamation of Mk 16.6 that 'he has been
raised' is preceded by the naming of Jesus as the Crucified One. Even

1.   This pattern is particularly clear in Mk 16.6. The death of Jesus is presented
through substantive use of the participle, creating a title: he is the Crucified One
(τὸν ἐσταυρωμένον). In contrast the resurrection is presented as an action done
upon Jesus: he has been raised (ἠγέρθη).

the references in Mk 9.9-10 have some connection to Jesus' death. In the following scene the disciples are reminded that the Son of Man will suffer and be treated with contempt (Mk 9.12). This scene is framed by two passion predictions (8.31; 9.31). In this way the narrative establishes an inviolable bond between the raising of Jesus and the abuse and torture which ended his life.

The grammatical constructions behind this image suggest a further association. While two different stems are employed (ἀνίστημι in 8.31; 9.31; 10.9, 10, 33-34; ἐγείρω in 14.28; 16.6), and different verbal forms are used (the aorist infinitive in 8.31; 9.10; 14.28; the future in 9.31; 10.34; the aorist indicative in 9.9; 16.6), each instance bears a passive or intransitive form. In this way the focus falls not upon what Jesus does, but upon what is done to Jesus. These terms likely point to divine initiative in the raising of Jesus.

The effect of these patterns of construction is important. The raising of Jesus is presented more in terms of his destiny than his status. His raising is not an abstracted act of exaltation; it is God's response to the violent death which Jesus endured. This subtle and nuanced pattern of characterization sets the tone for every naming of Jesus as the Risen One. As a consequence of this strategy the image of Jesus as the Risen One can never become an ontological description of status abstracted from the story of his life and death. The Gospel of Mark presents no resurrection appearances, and it wraps the story of transfiguration (Mk 9.2-10) in a cloak of secrecy (9.9-10). Consequently, triumphalistic theology can hardly be sketched around this image of Jesus as the Risen One. In the Gospel of Mark the raising of Jesus represents the act of God in response to the torture and injustice which ended the life of Jesus. In this manner the narrative constructs a sober definition around the image of Jesus as the Risen One.

This technique further demonstrates the complex narrative patterns employed in the naming of Jesus. There is no real background to the role of Jesus as the Risen One, and the term never becomes a title in the Gospel of Mark. Nonetheless, the image of the smitten Jesus as one raised by God plays a key role in the naming of Jesus.

Chapter 17

THE CRUCIFIED ONE

> But he says to them, 'Do not be afraid. You are seeking Jesus the Naz-
> arene, the Crucified One. He has been raised. He is not here' (Mk 16.6).

The naming of Jesus as the Crucified One (τὸν ἐσταυρωμένον)[1] in Mk
16.6 provides the barest form of titular Christology. This title has no
background as a messianic term or even as a common description.
Indeed, its focus is inherently anti-messianic. The title has no inherent
value that is unique, for thousands of Jews were crucified at the hands
of Rome, many for criminal activity. Even within the Gospel of Mark,
the cross has not been developed as an explicitly christological symbol.[2]

At the same time the naming of Jesus as the Crucified One provides a
complex pattern of titular Christology. The title is used once of Jesus in
the last scene of the story (16.6). It is associated with the empty tomb
(16.5), with the naming of Jesus as the Nazarene (16.6), and with the
promised appearance of Jesus (16.7). This title is confirmed by its
location and by the external witness of the messenger (16.5). The title
thus occupies a profoundly enigmatic position: the most solitary of all
titles in the Gospel of Mark stands at the climactic point of the story.

It is precisely this position which demonstrates the value of the title
Crucified One and the profound power of narrative worlds. The Risen
One who goes before the disciples into Galilee and the future is defined
by the story of his past. He is no creation of the wounded psyche, no

---

1. A similar linguistic form is found in the naming of John as the Baptist
(ὁ βαπτίζων in Mk 1.4) and the naming of Judas as the betrayer (ὁ παραδιδούς in
Mk 14.42).

2. Prior to Mk 14–16 the term is used only once (Mk 8.34); here it refers to
discipleship rather than Christology. In the passion story (Mk 14–16) the symbolic
value of the cross is not developed. Consequently, every effort must be made to
avoid the importation of Pauline Christology and later credal developments into
this narrative.

product of misguided enthusiasm, no specter of religious need. The
Gospel of Mark declares that disciples may meet the risen Lord only as
the Crucified One. Even this image is removed from the realm of
abstraction and speculation, for the identity of the Crucified One is
defined in the life of Jesus, the Nazarene. The status of the Crucified
One is formed wholly and exclusively through the story which begins
with the naming of Jesus (1.1) and proceeds through the journey of the
Nazarene (1.9; 1.24; 10.47; 14.67; 16.6). Conversely, the story of Jesus
reaches its necessary climax and consummation in his destiny as the
Crucified One. This narrative construct joins the pieces of this Gospel
into an indissoluble whole: the story of Jesus cannot be understood
apart from its consummation in the cross, the destiny of Jesus is rooted
in the contours of his journey, the Risen One who goes before the
Church bears the objective figure of Jesus, the Crucified Nazarene.

The pattern and placement of this title are no accident; they belong to
the formal logic of this narrative. Building upon the history of Jesus
and the hope of the Church, the title of Crucified One consummates the
naming of Jesus within this story. The construction of narrative images
and the production of kerygmatic claim converge in the last scene of
this performance: the Risen One who goes before is none other than
Jesus the Nazarene, the Crucified One. This is his story, this is his destiny, this is his name.

Chapter 18

CONCLUSION

And they feared a great fear and were saying to themselves, 'Who then
is this...?' (Mk 4.41).

It becomes evident, following a controlled analysis, that the Gospel of
Mark does not simply import a few prepackaged titles which are inherently messianic to articulate its view of Jesus. On the contrary, the
Gospel of Mark shapes and reshapes numerous images into a stream of
titular Christology. This construction of names for Jesus is one element
in a larger, more complex strategy of characterization. The processes
through which the Gospel of Mark gives names to Jesus provide one
key to its presentation of the Christian kerygma.

Titular Christology: Content

The description of Jesus through various titles and images adds dimension, nuance and energy to his profile. *What* these names say about
Jesus is noteworthy.

Jesus the Nazarene

The Nazarene imagery has no historical or symbolic background, and it
appears only five times within this Gospel. The Gospel of Mark
confirms this title and fills out its content through various associations:
Jesus is the Son who bears the Spirit; he is the Holy One of God who
drives out demons; he is the Son of David; he is the Teacher who has
mercy to heal and authority to call disciples; he is rejected, abandoned,
betrayed, abused, killed; he is the Crucified and Risen One who goes
before the community. The value of this description is created through
its location at strategic junctures of Jesus' story: at the beginning (1.9,
24), in the context of the passion (10.47; 14.67), on the day of his
resurrection (16.6). At the end of the story the Nazarene title is

connected to Jesus' destiny as the Crucified One (16.6). In this way the story of Jesus' life culminates in his passion, and his identity as the Crucified One is undergirded by the whole of his life story.

Prophet

The portrait of Jesus as God's Prophet operates against the backdrop of a broad, complex historical background. Any prophetic Christology behind the synoptic tradition seems to have been largely suppressed, replaced or incorporated, and prophetic Christology played no central role in the ongoing development of Christian thought. In contrast to this pattern of development, the Gospel of Mark confirms Jesus as the Prophet. It does so without making direct confessional use of the term. This title belongs to the popular speculation about Jesus, but it also presents Jesus as the rejected Prophet who will die in Jerusalem. Within the passion story the instruction, prediction and suffering of Jesus demonstrate his prophetic role, and these traits converge in the saying of Mk 10.45. Beginning with his rejection in his home town, Jesus' itinerant ministry and his shameful death are sketched throughout as the story of God's rejected Prophet.

The Greater One

The description of Jesus as the Greater One has no historical background, but belongs exclusively to the relationship between Jesus and John the Baptist. While John comes before Jesus, the priority of Jesus and his mission are established in the preaching of John himself. The effect of this construction is to characterize Jesus as the Prophet whose mission marks the culmination of the prophetic tradition.

Priest

The priestly images of Jesus do not stand in continuity with the Melchizedek speculation in its background. Within the Gospel of Mark the title is never used of Jesus, but priestly images are developed around Jesus' conflict with the religious leaders. This priestly Christology flows directly into the passion story and generates a unique understanding of Jesus' ministry, particularly in light of the fall of Jerusalem and the Temple.

King

While the King title represents a clear messianic expectation within the Old Testament, within Judaism, and within early Christianity, this term is abandoned by the Gospel of Mark. Applied to Jesus only by his critics in view of his execution, the King title serves no positive role as a description of Jesus. It belongs more properly to those who instigate violence, first against the Baptist, then against Jesus and his followers.

Teacher

While teaching with wisdom is a trait found in various forms of messianic expectation, there seems no precedent for understanding the Messiah as Teacher, and this title played little role in the Christology of the early Church. In contrast to these developments the Gospel of Mark generates and confirms the portrait of Jesus as the Teacher. This title is associated with images of wonder and power, but also with the controversy which leads to Jesus' death. The title of Teacher is enriched through non-titular descriptions of his teaching ministry. As a consequence the image of the wondrous Teacher whose ministry ends in death provides a central element in the characterization of Jesus.

Shepherd

The shepherd imagery of the Old Testament is connected eventually to Davidic descriptions and consequently to messianic expectations. Through citations from the Old Testament the Gospel of Mark picks up on this imagery without embracing its Davidic aspects. In this way a new line of interpretation is opened. The Gospel of Mark presents Jesus as the Shepherd who cares for God's flock, which has been abandoned by its leaders. In a realignment of Old Testament tradition, Jesus is consistently portrayed as the Shepherd who is smitten and abandoned. In a novel development upon Old Testament prophecy, Jesus is also portrayed as the Risen One who will reconstitute the scattered flock of God. This pattern of critical interaction and realignment generates a unique description of Jesus and his ministry.

Holy One of God

The Holy One of God is a singular description of Jesus which has no real background. Its association with Jesus' activity as exorcist is not exploited, and miracle stories are drawn into a larger strategy of characterization. While the Holy One title is not omitted, its potential is not developed. As a consequence this title remains isolated and largely inconsequential in the naming of Jesus.

Suffering Servant of God

The Suffering Servant does not provide a clear messianic image or expectation in the Old Testament or in pre-Christian Judaism. While this title is never used of Jesus in the Gospel of Mark, the passion story employs images and allusions from the Servant tradition. In light of this connection the Servant imagery may be seen at work in the baptism scene. Mark 10.45 draws upon this opening characterization, and the vineyard parable evokes similar images (Mk 12.1-12). Jesus' service unto death is given titular expression in the closing scene (16.1-8). The Servant imagery is thus a passion metaphor which moves outward from the scenes of Jesus' death to encompass the whole of his story.

Son of David

The Son of David title carries clear messianic expectations within the Old Testament, within Judaism and within early Christianity. The Gospel of Mark makes limited use of this title within a narrow segment of its story. In contrast to the background of this title, the Gospel of Mark associates the Son of David with the extraordinary mercy of Jesus and with his authority over Davidic traditions, including Jerusalem and the Temple. The narrative neither confirms nor negates this title, and it undergoes no further development. In contrast to its heritage, Son of David plays little role in the naming of Jesus.

Son of God

While the Son of God title has an extensive background in the history of religions, it is difficult to demonstrate a clear messianic expectation around the Son of God title in the Old Testament or in pre-Christian Judaism. Nonetheless, Son of God is central to early Christian formulations. In the Gospel of Mark the portrait of Jesus as the Son of God stands at a crucial juncture between the generalized images of the historical background and the confessional certainty of early Christianity. The title is used eight times and is loosely associated with contrasting images of authority and suffering. The title is confirmed as a valid description, but it is employed primarily in the framework of Jesus' story. Through this construction the entire story of Jesus is offered as definition and demonstration of the claim that Jesus is God's Son.

Son of Man

Various Son of Man images seem to converge around the end of the first century CE into a Jewish expectation of a heavenly judge and deliverer. A pre-Christian origin for this expectation cannot be demonstrated, and this expectation may first arise with Jesus or the early Church. The Gospel of Mark stands within this developing tradition, but makes its own contribution.

The Son of Man is a frequent title in the Gospel of Mark, but it is confined mostly to the last half of the narrative. This title is associated with images of power and judgment, but also with suffering, service and death. This imagery is confirmed in the Gospel of Mark, but it is surrounded by both clarity and mystery. The title points ultimately to realms which lie beyond the scope of the narrative—the sovereignty of God and the claims of the future. As a consequence the use of the Son of Man title in the Gospel of Mark presents an unanswered riddle which keeps open the consummation of Jesus' story.

Lord

The background of the Lord title lies in secular usage, but at some undefined point the term came to have reference to Yahweh. Early Christianity made the confession of Jesus as Lord a central component of faith. The Gospel of Mark provides a historical and theological bridge between these two movements. While the title is not used of Jesus in a clear confessional way in the Gospel of Mark, various aspects of the narrative develop this imagery. The Lord title is used to refer both to Yahweh and to secular masters. A few metaphors combine these two traditions. One passage (Mk 12.35-37) draws upon Psalm 110 to make a christological statement, but no direct connection is made to Jesus. This christological use of the Lord title is functional, futuristic and monotheistic. Through various techniques this future lordship is connected to the work of Jesus and is laid across the story of his life. This delicate description of the lordship of Jesus provides one of the most primitive and authentic strands of Christology.

Christ

Pre-Christian images of the Messiah developed within the Old Testament around the promises to David and emerged in sharper focus within the thought of Judaism. These concepts center around an earthly political figure of Davidic descent who will usher in a new age. Beyond this the expectations of a Messiah are marked by wide-ranging diversity and ambiguity. The Gospel of Mark gives clearer definition to its messianic understanding, but it does so through an unusual technique. Of the eight appearances of this title, four have direct reference to Jesus (1.1; 8.29; 14.61; 15.32). Since the description in 8.29 is silenced and the reference is 15.32 is derisive, the confessional use of the term belongs largely to the framework of the story. Jesus is confessed as Messiah in the opening lines of the narrative (1.1) and in his own statement before the high priest (14.61-62). Beyond these confessions the term is given no real development by the story line. Through this pattern the framework insists upon the importance of this title while the story line provides its substance. As a consequence the content of the Christ title is articulated through the various scenes which constitute the story of Jesus.

The Risen One

The Risen One is a term with no background. This non-titular description emerges from seven references to the destiny of Jesus and is associated with important images: the violent death of Jesus and the sovereign acts of God. This description of Jesus' destiny is tied precisely to the story of his death and limits triumphalistic conceptions.

The Crucified One

The title of Crucified One has no background and stands as an unadorned image at the end of Jesus' story. This climactic description stands alone, yet it is bolstered by the larger narrative strategy. The Crucified One is defined as none other than Jesus, who lived the concrete life of the Nazarene. In this manner the climactic image of the Crucified One gains its content from the whole of Jesus' story.

Summation

The narrative world of the Gospel of Mark proves a fertile seed-bed for descriptions of Jesus' worth. The content of this description is extensive and diverse. These images far exceed the bounds of pre-Christian messianic categories and expectations. At times the Gospel of Mark connects to these prior images, then extends their parameters. At other times prior developments and traditions are reversed. In some instances the Gospel of Mark strikes out on its own to create new descriptions of Jesus. Through various patterns of narrative construction the Gospel of Mark employs a host of images and names for Jesus. The blending of these varied narrative voices sustains a complex, multi-faceted portrait of Jesus.

Titular Christology: Process

The titular description of Jesus proves to be more than a collection of terms. In the naming of Jesus not only the content, but also the process prove to be important. Various patterns may be observed in the construction of Jesus' narrative profile.

Embedded Titles

Most titles make their major contribution to the story line. Some terms tend to be isolated and to make a limited contribution to the story: Holy One of God, Greater One, Son of David. Other images exert more extensive influence over the plotted sequence: Prophet, Priest, Teacher, Shepherd, Suffering Servant, Lord. The King title is considered, then rejected, within the flow of the story. Each of these images is embedded within the story line of this Gospel and gives substance to the story of Jesus.

Framework Titles

Other titles operate primarily within the framework of the Gospel. While the description of Jesus as Son of God is woven into the story line at a few points, it functions mostly as a framing device. This title belongs to the introduction to the Gospel (1.1), to its opening scene (1.11), and to its climactic confession (14.61-62). Through this construction the Son of God title provides a grid through which to read the various scenes of Jesus' life. Each twist and turn of Jesus' journey is now framed as the story of the Son of God.

This framing technique is more explicit in the Christ title. The term is used directly of Jesus on four occasions (1.1; 8.29; 14.61; 15.32). The saying in 8.29 is confined by a command to secrecy, and the saying in 15.32 is derisive. Mark 1.1 and 14.61 thus frame the story of Jesus with the confession that he is the Christ. This description is provided by the most trustworthy voices in the narrative world—those of the narrator and of Jesus. This pattern of construction insists that each element of Jesus' story be read within a christological framework. As a consequence scenes which carry no explicit christological value are drawn into the larger portrait of Jesus as the Christ of God.

Climactic Titles

Some titles gather the focus of the entire story into a climactic confession. The use of Christ and Son of God in Mk 14.61-62 provides a climactic moment, though these titles belong to a larger frame. The description of Jesus as the Crucified One (16.6) provides the one pure example of a climactic title. No content or definition is articulated around this term, and it remains inherently flat. Its role is to stand at the end of the narrative and to gather up the various streams of characterization. Because of this strategy the title of Crucified One provides the focal point for understanding every description of Jesus, and the claim that Jesus is the Crucified One is undergirded by each scene of his story.

Extending Titles

A few titles found within the story serve primarily to point beyond the narrative. The description of Jesus as the Risen One provides a bridge which moves the reader beyond the final scenes. In the days ahead, Jesus may be met by his followers in Galilee. While this promise moves beyond the bounds of the story line, this image is rooted in the details of the story: the Risen One is none other than Jesus, the Crucified Nazarene. In this way the narrative provides a bridge leading directly from the world of the story into the hope of the resurrection.

A more dramatic extension is provided in the Son of Man title. This imagery points to a reality which stands at some distance, both temporally and ideologically, from the realms of the story. At some point in the future and under the sovereign authority of God, the Son of Man will come with power and glory. This promise explodes the bounds of the story and leaves open the final destiny of its participants. In this way the disastrous scenes which end the life of Jesus and the oppression which surrounds the way of discipleship are cast against a cosmic background of divine hope. Nonetheless, this imagery may not become the source of unbridled speculation and enthusiasm. The Son of Man who comes at the end of the age has a prior history in Jesus of Nazareth. The images of authority and the suffering which surround the Son of Man within the narrative ground this hope in the story of Jesus. The story of God's future stands in sober continuity with the story of Jesus' past. It is precisely this story, the story of the Crucified Nazarene, which is opened to the redemptive hope of God's coming reign.

Titular Christology: Hermeneutics

A flurry of hermeneutical activity circulates around the titles. These narrative constructions provide key patterns through which to interpret Jesus and his story. On the other hand the titles are themselves the object of hermeneutical realignment.

Hermeneutics on the Titles

The titles which do have a background have not been absorbed into the Gospel of Mark as fixed christological definitions; they have been transformed and realigned through this process of induction. In some titles a clear pattern of extension is evident. The Old Testament shepherd imagery is realigned to focus the destiny of Jesus as one smitten and abandoned. The expectation of messianic wisdom is transformed into descriptions of Jesus as the Teacher. The theme of the suffering prophet is expanded. The Holy One title is framed in new perspective. The Suffering Servant is given messianic dimensions. The title of Lord is given christological perspective. A priestly Christology is defined from Old Testament images.

In contrast to this pattern of extension, other titles reduce their heritage. The shepherd imagery loses its Davidic aura. Militaristic images of the Messiah are abandoned. The Son of David expectations lose their political focus. Priestly Christology is sketched without reference to Melchizedek.

One pattern of reversal may be observed. The title of King is emptied in the Gospel of Mark of its messianic value. It points instead to leaders who instigate violence against the Baptist, against Jesus and against Jesus' followers.

A few images emerge as novel descriptions forged from the materials of Jesus' life. Nazarene terminology provides the collection point for various narrative traits, then links the story of Jesus to his destiny as the Crucified One. The description of Jesus as the Greater One defines his relation to John the Baptist and presents Jesus as the culmination of the prophetic tradition. The image of Jesus as the Risen One portrays the outcome of his suffering and provides a bridge to the experience of the Church. The naming of Jesus as the Crucified One occurs at the climax of the story of Jesus and gathers the varied elements of his story into coherent focus. In contrast to its background, the Son of Man title now provides a clear messianic image. These terms each represent novel descriptions generated in and around the stories of Jesus.

Thus, a wide range of hermeneutical moves is performed upon titles as they are sketched into the story of this Gospel. No titles are taken over as untouched, preconceived descriptions. Most images are reconceived in light of Jesus and woven into his story; some are extended, some reduced, some reversed. Some titles are first conceived within the project of Mark's Gospel and its naming of Jesus.

Hermeneutics of the Titles

The titles exert their own hermenutical impact. The world of the narrative is defined and maintained through the various codes they set out. Likewise, the reader's evaluation is guided and obedience is demanded through these canons of interpretation. As a consequence titular Christology provides a strategic component in the performance and demand of this narrative. These constructive patterns represent literary codes with distinct theological significance.

Many titles connect the story of Jesus to the world of the Old Testament. The coherence of expectation and experience is demonstrated in various images: Suffering Servant, Son of David, Christ, Prophet, Priest, Shepherd, Son of God, Lord. Scholars usually give attention to the way in which Jesus fulfills these expectations. While this pattern is certainly at work in the Gospel of Mark, another hermeneutical transaction may be observed: the experience with Jesus provides a crucial hermeneutic through which to interpret Old Testament expectations. Thus, the suffering endured by Jesus is seen as a central messianic trait. David's Son is seen to be Lord over all Davidic tradition. The suffering of the Servant takes on messianic overtones. The Christ title is redefined according to the parameters of Jesus' story. Priestly Christology takes its parameters not from Melchizedek but from Jesus. The prophetic tradition is seen to culminate in the message of Jesus and in his violent death. Conceptions of the smitten shepherd are recast so that they bear the image of the crucified Jesus. In these and other ways the reality of Jesus provides the mold through which Old Testament images and expectations are recast and reconfigured in the naming of Jesus. He is the one who fits no formula.[1] In the Gospel of Mark Jesus provides

---

1. Eduard Schweizer coined this phrase. See *Jesus* (trans. D. Green; London: SCM Press, 1971 [1968]), pp. 13-51.

the *hermeneusis* of every title, and Christology becomes forevermore the story of Jesus.

Other titles create hermeneutical links between key aspects of Jesus' identity. This may be observed within the Son of Man title. The Son of Man who comes with cosmic glory at the end of the age is connected to the earthly Son of Man whose service was marked by authority and suffering. Various other links are established within this narrative. The Risen One who meets the Church in the future is the Crucified One who died in scandal and shame. The status of this Crucified One is defined by his identity as the Nazarene. The Shepherd who now leads the people of God and will be struck down is precisely the one who will go before the Church into Galilee. These links provide both continuity and correction. Jesus' story cannot be separated into isolated fragments with monolithic focus. The Christ cannot be experienced in the unbounded glory of wisdom or spiritual experience, for his status is forever bound to the story of Jesus.

Other titles represent a delicate negotiation between their own background, the reality of Jesus and the faith of the early Church. The enthusiastic confession of primitive Christianity that Jesus is Lord is framed in the Gospel of Mark in terms sensitive to its theological framework. The lordship of Jesus is affirmed within this Gospel, but it is done so in terms that are functional, futuristic and wholly monotheistic.

A similar pattern may be observed in the title Son of God. Standing between the ambiguity of its background and the confessional certainty of the early Church, the Gospel of Mark confirms this title within the perspective of Jesus' story. In a similar way, whatever lines of development lie behind the Son of Man have been rerouted through the events of Jesus' life and death.

The pattern observed in Old Testament images proves true of every description of Jesus. What Jesus said and did, as well as the destiny he experienced, all provide the interpretive grid through which to read various titles and descriptions. Ultimately, it is Jesus himself who provides the keys to interpretation of these descriptions. Jesus himself becomes the first hermeneusis of the titles.

The patterns at work in the naming of Jesus echo the larger christological strategy of this Gospel.[2] Traditional miracle stories have been realigned to demonstrate the authority of Jesus' teaching. Controversy

2.   See Broadhead, *Teaching with Authority*; and *Prophet, Son, Messiah*.

scenes lead to his arrest and execution. The passion story is grounded in the story of Jesus' life. The reciprocity and diversity which mark the portrait of Jesus throughout this Gospel are evident in the strategy behind the titles.

Titular Christology: History

The patterns through which the Gospel of Mark constructs a titular stream of Christology are ultimately literary constructs. Nonetheless, these patterns suggest an intriguing relationship with the history which surrounds these terms.

The History of Jesus

There seems to be some correlation between attempts to isolate titles used by Jesus and the manner of their presentation within the Gospel of Mark. Among the titles with the strongest historical connection to the ministry of Jesus may be Son of Man, Son of God, Servant of God.[3] Servant of God is more a set of characteristics and allusions than a confessional title in the Gospel of Mark, and Son of God serves primarily as a framework title. This supports those scholars who would argue that Jesus' activity implies such descriptions over against those who would claim these as self-descriptions by Jesus.

Historical hypothesis and literary technique cohere in the Son of Man title. This title, which is judged by many as the term most likely to have been used by Jesus, is Jesus' most frequent self-designation in the Gospel of Mark. It is found within the story exclusively on the lips of Jesus, and this term did not prove popular in Church confessions.

The History of Early Christianity

A stronger correspondence may be found between the narrative presentation of Jesus and the faith of the early Church. In the Gospel of Mark most titles are not statements *from* Jesus, but statements *about*

---

3.   For example, Cullmann believes that Servant, Son of Man, Son of God go back to veiled allusions in the ministry of Jesus. Ferdinand Hahn believes that Jesus was addressed as Teacher, Master, Lord in his own lifetime, but only in the sense of earthly authority. He believes that some of the futuristic Son of Man sayings go back to Jesus. Reginald Fuller believes that Jesus made only preliminary use of the Lord title, that he was conscious of a unique sonship, and that he understood himself in prophetic terms. These implicit christological elements were then developed by the early Church. Pokorný does not credit any of the titles to the earthly Jesus.

him. He is described as Lord, Teacher, the Greater One, the Holy One of God, King, Son of David, Crucified One, but only on the lips of others. He acknowledges his identity as Christ and as Son of God, but only in one scene near the end of his life. His only discussion of Christology is impersonal and abstract (Mk 12.35-37). The central focus of his message and his activity is not himself, but the kingdom of God (Mk 1.14-15). His central demand is not orthodox confession, but repentance and obedience (1.14-15, 16-20). A clear narrative pattern emerges: concern for christological clarity belongs more to those who surround him than to Jesus himself. This literary canon most likely presents an accurate reflection of the historical situation: the creeds, confessions and titles which highlight christological values belong more to the faith statements of the early Church about Jesus than to the message of Jesus himself.[4]

Further coherence between text and context may be identified. Some descriptions of Jesus are presented without titular confession, either by Jesus or those who follow him. No one within the story confesses Jesus as God's final Prophet, yet the narrative insists this image is accurate. The priestly activity of Jesus may be observed, but the title is never voiced. The destiny of Jesus as the Suffering Servant emerges through his activity rather than in titular claims. He is never called Shepherd, yet he embodies this imagery. Jesus is never confessed as the exalted Lord within this narrative, but authentic overtones of his lordship echo through his story. While the claim is never made that such terms were used by Jesus or even of Jesus, the narrative insists that these images are true of Jesus.

This pattern exhibits both caution and license. The Gospel of Mark reads primitive confessions onto the lips of Jesus with great reserve. In

---

4. Schweizer, *Jesus*, pp. 21-22, sees in this phenomenon a historical reality with crucial hermeneutical and theological implications: 'In any case, Jesus did not assume any current title with an exalted meaning... His refusal to use these titles shows that he fits none of these formulas. Repetition of a pre-existing title, assent to some definition of Jesus' nature, cannot dispense a man from real encounter with him... By his very act of avoiding all common labels, Jesus keeps free the heart of the man who encounters him. He wants to enter into this heart himself, in all the reality of what he does and says, not as an image already formed before he himself has a chance to encounter the person... after Easter a disciple can proclaim Jesus as Messiah, Son of God, Servant of God, and Son of Man; but when he does so, the name of Jesus does as much to define these concepts as the concepts do to suggest what Jesus is.'

distinction from the Fourth Gospel, Christology is never forced onto the agenda of Jesus. At the same time the Gospel of Mark does not limit its christological portrait to the language of Jesus. This Gospel employs interpretive license to articulate the significance of Jesus in new terms, concepts, titles, and images. Even as the words of Jesus were translated from his native tongue into the language of new hearers, so new descriptions of Jesus are forged from the story of his life. These descriptions represent a cautious negotiation between the traditions of the Old Testament, the reality of Jesus and the situation of early believers.[5] In this way the story of Jesus and his significance are recast and re-presented to subsequent generations and to changed situations. This interpretive process sustains the story of Jesus, yet ensures its relevance for changing times and places. The titular Christology presented within this Gospel seeks to maintain two lines of continuity; it seeks to preserve contact with both the historical events which produced these claims and the contemporary audiences who attend these stories.

Titular Christology: Kerygma

While this narrative exhibits literary, hermeneutical and historical patterns, its central task is kerygmatic. The Gospel of Mark exhibits no self-awareness of its identity apart from its kerygmatic claims. The narrative presents itself as a Gospel—a message of good news (Mk 1.1). The story is about the message which Jesus himself preached—the gospel of God (1.14-15). This preaching activity characterizes the daily ministry of Jesus (1.38-39). Proclamation also belongs to the task of discipleship (5.19-20; 6.12-13). The final command of this Gospel is to announce the story about Jesus (16.7). Ultimately the gospel is to be proclaimed in all of the world (13.10; 14.9). Titular Christology and all other constructions must be read within this defining trait. The naming of Jesus within this Gospel is not primarily an exercise in history, hermeneutics or literature. Ultimately the naming of Jesus within this Gospel is a kerygmatic presentation and a kerygmatic claim. While the reader may reject or accept these demands, this kerygmatic profile remains the defining trait of this narrative.

---

5.   Thus, Jesus is defined as the Priest of God who fulfills Old Testament values and leads God's people into the future.

Summation

At the end of this study several aspects of the titles for Jesus come into view. Even a summary of the historical background behind the various titles makes it clear how little we know of the prehistory of such terms. It is difficult to draw direct lines between the background of any one title to its use in the ministry of Jesus or in the faith of the Church. It also becomes evident that such connections do not provide the sole methodological key to these titles. While the historical search must continue, the historical background of the titles proves less obvious and less useful than previously thought.

A similar situation arises around the consciousness of Jesus and his identification of himself. No single title can be demonstrated as indicative of Jesus' self-understanding. The manner in which Jesus understood and described himself lies beyond the limits of our current data and beyond the reach of present methodologies. While it is quite possible that Jesus did articulate his identity in various forms, the parameters of this presentation are not demonstrable. Most scholars now prefer to speak of implied Christology and self-awareness in the life of Jesus, but no single term of reference can be shown. It also becomes evident that titles do not stand or fall with the question of their use by Jesus. Since the purpose of such images is confessional rather than reconstructive, there need be no direct linguistic correlation between confessions about Jesus and confession from Jesus. That which is true about Jesus may be properly stated in terms that do not originate from Jesus. The validation of the titles lies not in their point of origin, but in their ability to communicate the reality to which they point.

These traits make it clear that the titles belong to a task which is larger than the telling of historical data or the echoing of words spoken by Jesus. These titles are part of a larger presentation and performance of the kerygma, the story of Jesus' role in the salvation of God. Titular Christology provides one strand in a much larger strategy which characterizes Jesus as the one in whom God has acted for human salvation. In order to communicate this message to a new time and place and people, this story is told in a language different from the language Jesus spoke (Greek rather than Aramaic) and in forms not used by the first believers (written narrative). These transitions are not a matter of reduction of some unblemished original; they represent instead a constructive strategy of communication and evangelism. It should come as no surprise, then, that the first written Gospel has at its core a titular Christology which draws upon various images and terms in the naming of Jesus. These terms and this strategy belong to the kerygmatic identity and purpose of this Gospel.

This strategy provides not only kerygmatic presentation and performance; it also presents kerygmatic claim. The manner and the content of this narrative insist upon hearing and obedience. The reader is not simply the target of selected information, but becomes the object of evangelism. The titular Christology constructed in this Gospel prescribes both hearing and discipleship.

While this study has been largely descriptive in its attention to the text, this Gospel demands more than hearing. Observation of the process by which early Christianity spoke of Jesus calls attention to our own patterns of enunciation. This story maintains its status as gospel only as it is translated and interpreted, transposed and transformed for each new context. While the task of hearing the primitive voice of the gospel calls for insight and clarity, the task of re-presenting the gospel calls for the added gifts of conviction and courage. The process of naming Jesus is an ongoing challenge confronting every generation, every tongue, every people.

Epilogue

It is not true that preconceived titles provide the lens through which to understand and articulate the significance of Jesus. It is more true that the experience and memory of Jesus within the early Church provided the scale upon which titles were measured, then abandoned or embraced. Jesus himself provides the hermeneusis of the various expectations and titles. At the same time, the experience and memory of Jesus provided the catalyst for production of a titular stream of Christology. This stream was never exclusive or predominant, but was woven into the larger portrait of Jesus. Titular Christology belongs to the larger frame of interpretation, to the wider experience of faith and to the task which predominates in the early Church—the presentation and performance of the kerygma.

Ancient Judaism brought its children to the Temple for a rite of dedication. This practice was taken up in different form within Christian tradition. Despite the divide at the time of the Reformation over the role of baptism, most traditions maintain some form of infant dedication. This ceremony is associated with publication of the name by which the newborn will be known. This presentation and naming before God gives clear articulation to who the child is, to what family and people the child belongs, to the hopes which surround the child. This process is seen as a public expression of the child's place within a Christian community of faith; thus it came to be known as *christening*.

This is a metaphor for the process at work in the naming of Jesus. The description of Jesus in the Gospel of Mark through various titles and images is ultimately a statement of faith and hope. Jesus' relationship to God is clarified through his role in God's salvation. His words and his deeds are recalled in the context of the kingdom of God. His call to salvation and service is remembered, the hope of his future is embraced, and his story is proclaimed to a new situation. Consequently, the naming of Jesus within this Gospel is a *christening* and a *christologizing*; it declares to a new generation the good news which attends his name.

BIBLIOGRAPHY

Achtemeier, Paul, *Mark* (Proclamation Commentaries; Philadelphia: Fortress Press, 1975).
—'Origin and Function of the Pre-Marcan Miracle Catenae', *JBL* 91 (1972), pp. 198-221.
Aune, David E., *Prophecy in Early Christianity and the Ancient Mediterranean World* (Grand Rapids: Eerdmans, 1983).
Bardy, G., 'Melchisedek dans la tradition patristique', *RB* 35 (1926), pp. 496-509; 36 (1927), pp. 25-45.
Bentzen, Aage, *King and Messiah* (Oxford: Basil Blackwell, rev. edn, 1970).
Bieler, L., *Theios Anēr: Das Bild des 'Göttlichen Menschen' in Spätantike und Frühchristentum* (Darmstadt: Wissenschaftliche Buchgesellschaft, 1967).
Blenkinsopp, J., *Prophecy and Canon: A Contribution to the Study of Jewish Origin* (Notre Dame: University of Notre Dame Press, 1977).
—'Prophecy and Priesthood in Josephus', *JJS* 25 (1974), pp. 239-62.
Bornkamm, G., *Jesus of Nazareth* (trans. I. McLusky and F. McLusky; London: Hodder & Stoughton, 1960 [1956]).
Bousset, W., *Kyrios Christos: A History of the Belief in Christ from the Beginnings of Christianity to Irenaeus* (trans. J. Steely; Nashville: Abingdon Press, 1970 [1913]).
Bousset, W., and H. Gressmann, *Die Religion des Judentums im spät-hellenistischen Zeitalter* (HNT, 21; Tübingen: J.C.B. Mohr, 3rd edn, 1926).
Braun, H., *Qumran und das Neue Testament* (2 vols.; Tübingen: J.C.B. Mohr [Paul Siebeck], 1966).
Broadhead, Edwin K., 'Mark 1,44: The Witness of the Leper', *ZNW* 83 (1992), pp. 257-65.
—*Prophet, Son, Messiah: Narrative Form and Function in Mark 14–16* (JSNTSup, 97; Sheffield: JSOT Press, 1994).
—*Teaching with Authority: Miracles and Christology in the Gospel of Mark* (JSNTSup, 74; Sheffield: JSOT Press, 1992).
—'Which Mountain Is "This Mountain"? A Critical Note on Mark 11.22-25', *Paradigms* 2.1 (1986), pp. 33-38.
Bultmann, Rudolf, *History of the Synoptic Tradition* (trans. John Marsh; New York: Harper & Row, rev. edn, 1963).
—*Theology of the New Testament* (2 vols.; trans. K. Grobel; London: SCM Press, 1952 [1948]).
Burger, Christoph, *Jesus als Davidssohn: Eine traditionsgeschichtliche Untersuchung* (Göttingen: Vandenhoeck & Ruprecht, 1970).
Collins, J.J., *The Apocalyptic Imagination: An Introduction to the Jewish Matrix of Christianity* (New York: Crossroad, 1989).
Colpe, C., 'ὁ υἱός τοῦ ἀνθρώπου', *TDNT*, VIII, pp. 400-77.
Conzelmann, H., *An Outline of the Theology of the New Testament* (trans. J. Bowden; London: SCM Press, 1969 [1968]).

Crenshaw, J.L., *Prophetic Conflict: Its Effect upon Israelite Religion* (Berlin: W. de Gruyter, 1971).

Cullmann, Oscar, *The Christology of the New Testament* (trans. S. Guthrie and C. Hall; London: SCM Press, 1963 [1957]).

Dalman, G., *The Words of Jesus Considered in the Light of Post-Biblical Jewish Writings and the Aramaic Language* (trans. D. Kay; Edinburgh: T. & T. Clark, 1902).

DeVries, S.J., *Prophet against Prophet: The Role of the Micaiah Narrative (1 Kings 22) in the Development of Early Prophetic Tradition* (Grand Rapids: Eerdmans, 1978).

Dibelius, M., *From Tradition to Gospel* (trans. B. Woolf; Cambridge: James Clarke, 1971 [1919]).

Donahue, John R., *Are You the Christ? The Trial Narrative in the Gospel of Mark* (SBLDS, 10; Missoula, MT: University of Montana Press, 1973).

—'Recent Studies on the Origin of "Son of Man" in the Gospel', *CBQ* 48 (1986), pp. 484-98.

Dunn, J.D.G., *Christology in the Making: A New Testament Inquiry into the Origins of the Doctrine of Incarnation* (Philadelphia: Westminster Press, 1980).

Fiebig, P., *Jüdische Wundergeschichten des neutestamentlichen Zeitalters, unter besonderer Berücksichtigung ihres Verhältnisses zum Neuen Testament bearbeitet: Ein Beitrag zum Streit um die 'Christusmythe'* (Tübingen: J.C.B. Mohr, 1911).

Fitzmyer, J., *A Wandering Aramean: Collected Aramaic Essays* (Missoula, MT: Scholars Press, 1979), pp. 143-60.

—'Another View of the "Son of Man" Debate', *JSNT* 4 (1979), pp. 58-68.

—'The Contribution of Qumran Aramaic to the Study of the New Testament', *NTS* 20 (1973–74), pp. 382-407.

—*The Gospel According to Luke* (AB, 28; Garden City, NY: Doubleday, 1981).

—*Responses to 101 Questions on the Dead Sea Scrolls* (New York: Paulist Press, 1992).

Förster, W., 'κύριος', *TDNT*, III, pp. 1034-58.

Frankfort, H., *Kingship and the Gods* (Chicago: University of Chicago Press, 1948).

Fuller, R.H., *The Foundations of New Testament Christology* (London: Lutterworth, 1965).

—*The Mission and Achievement of Jesus* (London: SCM Press, 1954).

Gadd, C.J., *Ideas of Divine Rule in the Ancient East* (London: Oxford University Press, 1948).

Grundmann, W., F. Hesse, A. van der Woude and M. de Jonge, 'χρίω', *TDNT*, IX, pp. 493-580.

Guthrie, Donald , *New Testament Theology* (Leicester: Inter-Varsity Press, 1981).

Hahn, Ferdinand, *The Titles of Jesus in Christology: Their History in Early Christianity* (trans. H. Knight and G. Ogg; London: Lutterworth, 1969 [1963]).

Heitmüller, W., 'Zum Problem Paulus und Jesus', *ZNW* 13 (1912), pp. 320-37.

Hengel, M., 'Jesus als messianischer Lehrer Weisheit und die Anfänge der Christologie', in *Sagesse et religion: Colloque de Strasbourg (octobre 1976)* (Bibliothèque d'Etudes Supérieures spécialisé d'Histoire des Religions de Strasbourg; Paris, 1979), pp. 147-88.

Hooker, Morna, *Jesus and the Servant* (London: SPCK, 1959).

—*The Son of Man in Mark* (London: SPCK, 1967).

Isaac, E., '1 (Ethiopic Apocalypse of) Enoch', *OTP*, I, pp. 5-89.

James, M.R., *The Apocryphal New Testament* (Oxford: Clarendon Press, 1924).

Jeremias, Gert, *Der Lehrer der Gerechtigkeit* (Göttingen: Vandenhoeck & Ruprecht, 1963).

Jeremias, J., *The Problem of the Historical Jesus* (trans. N. Perrin; Philadelphia: Fortress Press, 1977 [1957]).

—''Ηλ(ε)ίας', *TDNT*, II, pp. 934-41.

—'παῖς θεοῦ', *TDNT*, V, pp. 677-717.

Jerome, F.J., 'Das geschichtliche Melchisedek-Bild und seine Bedeutung im Hebräerbrief' (unpublished doctoral dissertation, Freiburg University, 1927).

Jonge, M. de, 'χρίω', *TDNT*, IX, pp. 509-17, 520-21.

Kähler, Martin, *The So-Called Historical Jesus and the Historic, Biblical Christ* (trans. C. Braaten; Philadelphia: Fortress Press, 1964 [1892]).

Karrer, Martin, *Der Gesalbte: Die Grundlagen des Christustitels* (Göttingen: Vandenhoeck & Ruprecht, 1990).

Käsemann, E., *Das wandernde Gottesvolk: Eine Untersuchung zum Hebräerbrief* (Göttingen: Vandenhoeck & Ruprecht, 1939).

Keck, Leander, 'Mark 3.7-12 and Mark's Christology', *JBL* 84 (1965), pp. 341-48.

Kelber, Werner, 'From Passion Narrative to Gospel', in *idem* (ed.), *The Passion in Mark: Studies on Mark 14–16* (Philadelphia: Fortress Press, 1976), pp. 153-80.

—*The Kingdom in Mark: A New Place and a New Time* (Philadelphia: Fortress Press, 1974).

Kertelge, Karl, *Die Wunder Jesu im Markusevangelium: Eine redaktionsgeschichtliche Untersuchung* (SANT, 23; Munich: Kösel, 1970).

Kingsbury, Jack D., *The Christology of Mark's Gospel* (Philadelphia: Fortress Press, 1983).

Koch, Dietrich-Alex, *Die Bedeutung der Wundererzählungen für die Christologie des Markusevangelium* (Berlin: W. de Gruyter, 1975), pp. 180-93.

Kümmel, W., *The New Testament: The History of the Investigation of its Problems* (trans. S. Gilmour and H. Kee; Nashville: Abingdon Press, 1972 [1970].

Kuhn, K.G., 'The Two Messiahs of Aaron and Israel', in K. Stendahl (ed.), *The Scrolls and the New Testament* (London: SCM Press, 1958), pp. 54-64.

Lindars, B., *Jesus Son of Man: A Fresh Examination of the Son of Man Sayings in the Gospels* (London: SPCK, 1983).

Lohse, E., *Märtyrer und Gottesknecht* (FRLANT, 64; Göttingen: Vandenhoeck & Ruprecht, 1966).

—*The New Testament Environment* (London: SCM Press, 1976 [1974]).

—' υἰὸς Δαυίδ', *TDNT*, VIII, pp. 481-82.

Luz, Ulrich, 'Das Geheimnismotiv und die markinische Christologie', *ZNW* 56 (1965), pp. 9-30.

Mack, Burton, *Mark and Christian Origins: A Myth of Innocence* (Philadelphia: Fortress Press, 1988).

Marshall, I.H., *Jesus the Saviour: Studies in New Testament Theology* (London: SPCK, 1990).

Martitz, W. von, 'υἰός', *TDNT*, VIII, pp. 336-40.

Meyer, R., 'προφήτης', *TDNT*, VI, pp. 796-828.

Mowinckel, Sigmund, *He That Cometh* (trans. G. Anderson; Oxford: Basil Blackwell, 1959 [1951]).

Mussner, F., 'Ein Wortspiel in Mk 1,24?', *BZ* NF 4 (1960), pp. 285-86.

Nickelsburg, George, 'Son of Man', *ABD*, VI, p. 137.

Perrin, N., 'Towards an Interpretation of the Gospel of Mark', in H.D. Betz (ed.), *Chris-*

tology and a Modern Pilgrimage: A Discussion with Norman Perrin (Missoula, MT: Scholars Press, rev. edn, 1974), pp. 1-78.

Pesch, Rudolf, *Das Markusevangelium* (HTKNT; 2 vols.; Freiburg: Herder, 3rd edn, 1980).

—*Der Prozess Jesu geht Weiter* (Freiburg: Herder, 1988).

Petersen, N., *Literary Criticism for New Testament Critics* (Philadelphia: Fortress Press, 1978).

Pokorný, Petr, *The Genesis of Christology: Foundations for a Theology of the New Testament* (trans. M. Lefebure; Edinburgh: T. & T. Clark, 1987 [1985]).

Rad, Gerhard von, *Old Testament Theology* (2 vols.; trans. D. Stalker; Edinburgh: Oliver & Boyd, 1965 [1960]).

Reumann, John, 'Jesus and Christology', in E. Epp and G. MacRae (eds.), *The New Testament and its Modern Interpreters* (Atlanta: Scholars Press, 1989), pp. 501-506.

Rhoads, D., and D. Michie, *Mark as Story: An Introduction to the Narrative of a Gospel* (Philadelphia: Fortress Press, 1982).

Riesner, Rainer, *Jesus als Lehrer: Eine Untersuchung zum Ursprung der Evangelien-Überlieferung* (Tübingen: J.C.B. Mohr [Paul Siebeck], 3rd edn, 1988).

Robertson, A.T., *A Grammar of the Greek New Testament in the Light of Historical Research* (Nashville: Broadman, 1934).

Schaeder, H.H., 'Ναξαρηνός, Ναξωραῖος', *TDNT*, IV, pp. 874-79.

Schenke, Ludger, *Die Wundererzählungen des Markusevangeliums* (Stuttgart: Katholisches Bibelwerk, 1974).

Schille, Gottfried, *Die urchristliche Wundertradition: Ein Beitrag zur Frage nach dem irdischen Jesus* (Stuttgart: Calwer Verlag, 1967).

Schreiber, Johannes, 'Die Christologie des Markusevangeliums', *ZTK* 58 (1961), pp. 154-83.

Schweitzer, Albert, *The Mystery of the Kingdom of God: The Secret of Jesus' Messiahship and Passion* (New York: Macmillan, 1950 [1901]).

—*The Quest of the Historical Jesus: A Critical Study of its Progress from Reimarus to Wrede* (trans. W. Montgomery; London: A. & C. Black, 2nd English edn, 1911 [1906]).

Schweizer, Eduard, ' "Er wird Nazoräer heissen" (zu Mc 1.24; Mt 2.23)', in W. Eltester (ed.) *Judentum, Urchristentum, Kirche* (Festschrift J. Jeremias; Berlin: Alfred Töpelmann, 1964), pp. 90-93.

—*Jesus* (trans. D. Green; London: SCM Press, 1971 [1968]).

—*The Good News According to Mark* (Atlanta: John Knox Press, 1970).

—*Lordship and Discipleship* (London: SCM Press, 1960 [1955]).

—'υἱός', *TDNT*, VIII, pp. 354-57.

Sjöberg, E., *Jesus und der Menschensohn* (Festschrift A. Vögtle; ed. R. Pesch and R. Schnackenburg; Freiburg: Herder, 1975).

—*Der verborgene Menschensohn in den Evangelien* (Lund: C.W.K. Gleerup, 1955).

Stauffer, E., *New Testament Theology* (trans. J. Marsh; London: SCM Press, 1955 [1941]).

Steck, Odil Hannes, *Israel und das gewaltsame Geschick der Propheten: Untersuchungen zur Überlieferung des deuteronomistischen Geschichtsbildes im Alten Testament, Spätjudentum und Urchristentum* (WMANT, 23; Neukirchen–Vluyn: Neukirchener Verlag, 1967).

Strecker, G., 'The Kerygmata Petrou', in W. Schneemelcher (ed.), *New Testament Apocrypha* (2 vols.; Philadelphia: Westminster Press, 1965 [1964]), II, pp. 102-11.

Suhl, Alfred, *Die Funktion der alttestamentlichen Zitate und Anspielungen im Markus-evangelium* (Gütersloh: Gerd Mohn, 1965).

Teeple, H.M., *The Mosaic Eschatological Prophet* (JBLMS, 10; Philadelphia: Society of Biblical Literature, 1957).

Tödt, H.E., *The Son of Man in the Synoptic Tradition* (London: SCM Press, 1965 [1959]).

Tolbert, Mary Ann, *Sowing the Gospel: Mark's World in Literary-Historical Perspective* (Minneapolis: Fortress Press, 1989).

Trocmé, Etienne, *The Formation of the Gospel According to Mark* (London: SPCK, 1975 [1963]).

Vermes, G., *Jesus the Jew: A Historian's Reading of the Gospels* (London: Collins, 1973).

—'The "Son of Man" Debate', *JSNT* 1 (1978), pp. 19-32.

Walker, W., 'The Son of Man: Some Recent Developments', *CBQ* 45 (1983), pp. 584-607.

Weeden, T., *Mark: Traditions in Conflict* (Philadelphia: Fortress Press, 1971).

Woude, A. van der, 'χρίω', *TDNT*, IX, pp. 517-20, 521-27.

Wrede, William, *The Messianic Secret* (trans. J.C.G. Greig; Cambridge: James Clark, 1971 [1901]).

Wright, R.B., 'Psalms of Solomon', *OTP*, II, pp. 639-70.

Zimmerli, W., 'παῖς θεοῦ', *TDNT*, V, pp. 654-77.

Zimmerli, W., and J. Jeremias, *The Servant of God* (London: SCM Press, 1957 [1952]).

INDEXES

INDEX OF REFERENCES

OLD TESTAMENT

NEW TESTAMENT

Naming Jesus